Art in
Action

Credits

Cover: Illustration by Judy Sakaguchi.

Art and Production: Book Production Systems, Inc.

Illustrations: Janet Colby, Jennifer Hewitson, Jannine Muelchi, Jim Staunton, Debra Stein. All illustrators represented by Richard W. Salzman, Artist Representative.

Publisher's Photos: All photos by Johnny Johnson/Click Studios except as credited below. Key: (t) top, (c) center, (b) bottom, (l) left, (r) right.

UNIT 1: Page viii(l), Corson Hirschfeld; viii(r), Mark Stephenson/West Light; 1, Paul Van Ginkel; 12, David Kraus; 17(l), Jeremiah S. Sullivan; 23(r), Image Bank West/Zad Longfield; 30, Tom McGuire; 32, Carl Purcell/Words and Pictures.

UNIT 2: Page 34(l), Tim Bieber; 34(r), Farrell Grehan/Photo Researchers, Inc.; 40, Ewing Galloway; 42, Bob Krist; 48, John Long; 52(l), Image Bank West/Art Wolfe; 52(r), Image Bank West/Joe Devenney; 53(l), Derek Fell; 53(r), Ewing Galloway; 55, Kurt Stier; 58, Image Bank West/Luis Castaneda; 59, Art Resource, NY; 61, Art Resource, NY; 64(l), Lee Boltin; 64(r), Eliot Elisofon; 66, Joseph A. DiChello, Jr.

UNIT 3: Page 69, Lee Boltin; 72, D.C. Lowe/Aperture Photobank; 80, Carmelo Guadagno; 83, Richard Todd; 91, Lee Boltin; 92(r), NASA; 95(l), Albert Moldauy/Art Resource, NY; 95(r), Image Bank West/Francisco Hidalgo; 98, Bill Ross/West Light; 100(l), 100(r), Lee Boltin.

UNIT 4: Page 102, Arthur Meyerson; 106, Derek Fell; 107, Courtesy of Biltmore Estate; 110(l), Image Bank West/Ted Mahiey; 110(r), David Langley; 111, Robert Llewellyn; 112, 113(t), Ewing Galloway; 113(b), David Muench; 114(t), Ewing Galloway; 114(b), Victor Englebert/Photo Researchers, Inc.; 115, Gary Braasch; 128(l), 128(r), Joe Baraban; 130, Walter Chandoha; 132(l), John Veltri/Photo Researchers, Inc.; 132(r), Rafael Macia/Photo Researchers, Inc.; 133(l), Michael Putnam/Peter Arnold, Inc.; 133(r), Tompix/Peter Arnold, Inc.; 134, Tom McGuire.

Art in Action

Guy Hubbard
Indiana University

Contributing Educators:

D. Sydney Brown
Lee C. Hanson
Barbara Herberholz

CORONADO PUBLISHERS
San Diego   Orlando   Dallas   Chicago

Requests for permission to make copies of any part of the work should be mailed to: Coronado Publishers, Inc., 1250 Sixth Avenue, San Diego, CA 92101

ACKNOWLEDGMENTS

For permission to reprint copyrighted material, grateful acknowledgment is made to the following:

PATRICIA AYERS FOR EVE MERRIAM: "Landscape" by Eve Merriam from *Finding A Poem* by Eve Merriam, copyright © 1970 by Eve Merriam.

Printed in the United States of America   ISBN 0-15-770048-8(3)

Table of Contents

Unit 1   What Is Art?   1

    1   Seeing Like an Artist   2
    2   Lines Are All Around Us!   4
    3   The Lines in Your Name   6
    4   Can You Feel It?   8
    5   Seeing with Your Fingers   10
    6   Feeling with Your Eyes   12
    7   Shapes Fit Together   14
    8   Seeing Forms in Buildings   16
    9   The Highs and Lows of Printing   18
   10   Seeing Colors in the World   20
   11   More Colors in the World   22
   12   Seeing Light in the World   24
   13   Colors Can Be Dark   26
   14   Art of the Orient   28
   15   Seeing Near and Far   30
        Exploring Art: Art Careers   32
        Review: Looking at Art   33

Unit 2   Working as an Artist   34

   16   Seeing Background and Foreground   36
   17   Seeing with Your Mind's Eye   38
   18   Art Can Fly!   40
   19   Does Your World Have   42
          Only One Color?
   20   Do You Feel Warm or Cool?   44
   21   What Is Cloth Made Of?   46
   22   Going 'Round and 'Round   48
   23   Lines Can Be Joined in Space   50
   24   Right Side, Left Side, or Both?   52
   25   Thumbs Up for Art   54
   26   By the Light of the Moon   56

27 Let's Get to the Important Part 58
28 Animals in Art 60
29 Give Your Finger a Face 62
30 Clothes Are Art, Too 64
  Exploring Art: Putting on a
   Puppet Show 66
  Review: Creating Art 67

Unit 3 The Many Faces of Art 68

31 Art That's Black and White 70
32 Art from Small Pieces 72
33 Animals Can Be Smooth 74
34 Canadian Indian Art 76
35 American Indian Art 78
36 Art That Tells Time 80
37 Art to Wear 82
38 Colorful Cloth 84
39 Layers and Layers of Crayon 86
40 Art That's Life-Sized 88
41 Chinese Paper Art 90
42 Your American Story 92
43 Art to Live In 94
44 Art That Shows Ideas and Feelings 96
45 Art That Moves 98
  Exploring Art: African Art 100
  Review: Knowing About Art 101

Unit 4 Art for Every Day 102

46 Art from Scraps 104
47 Garden in a Box 106
48 What Belongs in a Garden? 108
49 Pictures Help Poems 110
50 What Does a Desert Look Like? 112
51 What Belongs in a Desert? 114
52 Lines That Move 116

53 The Art of Advertising   118
54 Frame It!   120
55 Patterns for Fabrics   122
56 Spatter It!   124
57 Weaving, Looms, and Table Mats   126
58 Clowns Make You Laugh   128
59 What Kind of Artist Are You?   130
60 Putting on an Art Show   132
    Exploring Art: A Summer Diary   134
    Review: Valuing Art   135
    Glossary   **137**
    Artists' Reference   **141**
    Index   **143**

Unit 1

What Is Art?

What is art? Art is many things. Art is seeing, feeling, and thinking about the world. Art is telling others about the world. Through art you can tell about things by dancing, singing, painting, drawing, or showing your feelings in many other ways. Art lets you use your mind and all of your senses. What do your senses tell you about the picture on the left?

Art is also noticing the nice way all the parts of the world fit together. How do all the big and little parts fit together in these pictures?

As you learn about art you will begin to see as an artist. You will notice the important things artists see in the world. These things are called the **elements of art**. The elements of art are listed below. The picture above has examples of all the elements of art in it. Soon you will be able to find them in these pictures. You will see as an artist sees.

line	color
shape	space
texture	value

1 Seeing Like an Artist

Looking and Thinking

Art is all around you. It is easy to see if you know how to look. Sometimes you may need help. Maybe someone will notice something and show it to you. Perhaps someone will help you to look.

You can make a magic window that will help you to see art. By using the magic window, you can look at small pieces of the world around you. You will be able to show your eyes some fun things they need to see.

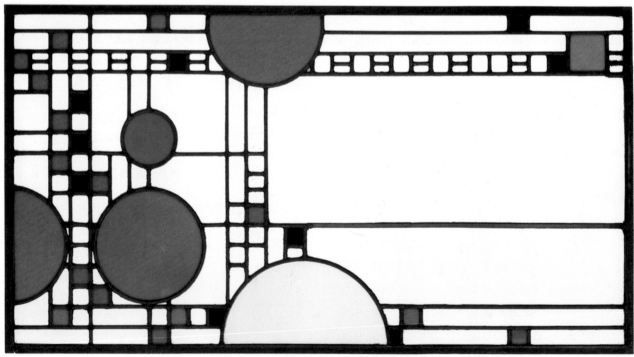

Frank Lloyd Wright, Window from the Coonley Playhouse, Riverside, Illinois, *1912, Leaded clear and cased glass, 18⅝" x 34³/₁₆". Collection, The Museum of Modern Art, New York, Joseph H. Heil Fund.*

Making Art

1. Lay the paper your teacher gives you on your desk or table. Take the right side of the paper and fold it to meet the left side. Press your thumb along the fold to make it stay. Now fold the bottom side to meet the top side. Press this fold to make it stay. Your paper should now be a small square.

2. You want to cut a small square window from the corner where all the folds meet. Fold up this corner to make a triangle about two fingers wide. Now take your scissors and cut off the triangle.

3. Unfold your paper. You have made a magic window. It will help you see art in the world.

4. Put your magic window over the picture on the left page. What do you see? Move the window slowly over the picture. Stop it when you see the color blue. Now look for square shapes. Can you see squares at the same time you see the color blue? Look for straight lines. Can you see straight lines at the same time you see circles? Move your magic window one last time. Write down all the shapes and colors you can see through it. See if someone else can see other shapes and colors.

Art Materials

Paper square

Scissors

THINK SAFETY

2 Lines Are All Around Us!

Looking and Thinking

Look at the palm of your hand. What do you see? Can you see all the different kinds of lines on your hand?

A fun part of learning about art is learning how to really see. When you first look at something, you see shapes and colors. To really see something as an artist sees it, you must look for the small parts, or **details**. **Lines** are important details of almost any thing.

The point of a pencil or pen can make a line. A stick pushed through sand makes a line. The edge of a paper is a line. If you hold up your pointing finger, you can make lines in space. With your finger, make a straight line. Try making zig-zag lines that look like the teeth of a saw. Now try other kinds of lines. The box below shows all kinds of lines.

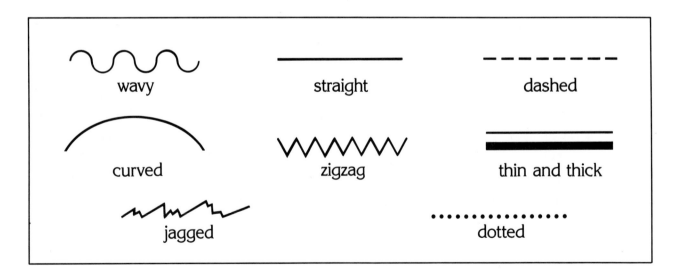

Look around you for other types of lines. Think where you have seen lines in nature. Close your eyes and think of trees, leaves, and spider webs.

Study this picture. How many different kinds of lines can you see?

Stuart Davis, New York Elevated. San Diego Museum of Art Collection.

Making Art

1. Use a pencil to practice making the kinds of lines shown in the box. Draw other types of lines you can see around you.

2. Now take your pencil and make lines that wander all over a fresh piece of paper. Go from one side of the paper to the other. Swing the pencil around in the middle of the paper. Bend and turn your lines to make interesting shapes and spaces.

3. Next, look for a space on your paper. Fill it in with one kind of line. It could be a line like one you made before, or it could be a new kind of line. Fill in many more spaces, until you have made a design of lines.

4. When you finish your design, share it with another person. Talk about all the different lines. Tell what they are like.

Art Materials

Pencil

Paper

3 The Lines in Your Name

Looking and Thinking

What kinds of lines do you use to write your name?
You might use curved lines and jagged lines, as well
as straight lines. Look how the name below is written.
Trace the lines of the name with your finger. What
kind of person do you think Annie is? Does how her
name is written make you think of her a certain way?

*Ed Ruscha, Annie, 1965, Oil on canvas,
22" x 20". Collection of Newport Harbor
Art Museum, Newport Beach, California,
Purchased by the Acquisition Council
with a Matching Grant from the National
Endowment for the Arts.*

Have you ever made a picture of your name? You
can make your name look the way you feel. You can
make the lines of your name sharp and pointy or soft
and curvy.

People in Mexico use yarn to make pictures called **nearikas**. This sun is a nearika. Notice how well the yarn lets you see the lines the artist used.

Making Art

1. You can make a nearika of your name. Think about the different kinds of lines and how they make you feel. Maybe curvy lines make you feel relaxed. Perhaps straight, solid lines tell more about how you feel.

2. Now make a pencil drawing of your name. Make it fill the whole page. Remember to make the letters wide so you can fill them in with yarn. Copy your drawing onto a thin piece of cardboard or a stiff piece of paper.

3. Choose yarn in your three favorite colors. Make sure the colors look good together. Cut the yarn into pieces that are easy to work with.

4. Use a squeeze bottle of glue to make a thin line of glue on the cardboard where you plan to put yarn. You will want to put the pieces of yarn closely together. Do not put glue on more than one letter at a time. (If glue is touched by air too long, it dries.) Carefully place the yarn on top of the glue line. Try to fill with yarn all the spaces formed by the letters.

5. Allow your nearika to dry. Did it turn out the way you wanted?

Art Materials
THINK SAFETY

Paper

Pencil

Cardboard or stiff paper

Glue

Yarn

Scissors

4 Can You Feel It?

Looking and Thinking

The **sculpture** on the next page was made nearly 2,500 years ago. We are lucky that we can still see this very old work of art.

Look at the lines on the sculpture. Notice the lines of the beard. The hair and robe also have many lines. How do these parts of the sculpture look? How do you think the sculpture would feel if you touched it? Would the lines in the beard make it feel rough? The way something feels when you touch it is called **texture**. Which parts of the sculpture have texture?

You can learn how to make lines and textures in sculpture by experimenting with clay. The artworks below were made by students like you. They learned how clay feels. They also learned how to use tools to give clay texture.

Making Art

1. Take a piece of clay and begin experimenting with it. How does it feel when you squeeze it? When you poke it? Can you pull pieces of it off? Can you put them back on?

2. Take the clay between your hands and squeeze it. Feel how it fits itself to your hands. Can you feel it filling in all the spaces of your hands?

3. Now let go of the clay. Can you see how your hands formed the clay a certain way? Your hands were the **mold** for the design you made. They formed a space which the clay filled up.

4. Now flatten the clay to make a small pancake. Choose several things you can use to make lines in the clay. Scissors, paper clips, and pencils are some useful tools. Hold each tool firmly, and press down on it to form interesting lines in the clay.

5. Run your fingers lightly over the clay when you are finished. How does it feel? See if someone at home can guess what you used to create the lines and textures.

Etruscan, Statuette of Zeus, 5th century B.C., Bronze, 6". The J. Paul Getty Museum. 55. AB. 12

Art Materials

Clay

Tools for making lines in clay

5 Seeing with Your Fingers

Looking and Thinking

Have you ever looked closely at a fish or held one in your hands? Most fish don't have smooth skin like people do. They have *scales*, or small rough pieces joined together.

Look at the fish below. Can you see its scales? How do you think the fish would feel to touch? How do you think the artist was able to show the scales so well?

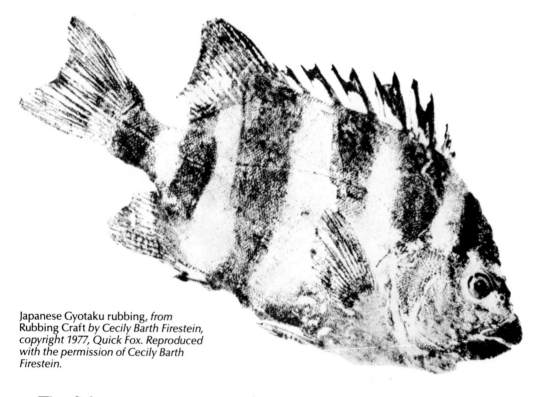

Japanese Gyotaku rubbing, *from* Rubbing Craft *by Cecily Barth Firestein, copyright 1977, Quick Fox. Reproduced with the permission of Cecily Barth Firestein.*

The fish you see was created by the art called **rubbing**. Rubbing lets you show texture, or the way something feels. Many things in nature have textures. Leaves, shells, and seeds are examples. Objects you use every day also have textures. Paper clips, buttons, and coins are examples. Can you think of other textured things you could show well with rubbings?

An artist your age created this rubbing. Can you name the things it shows?

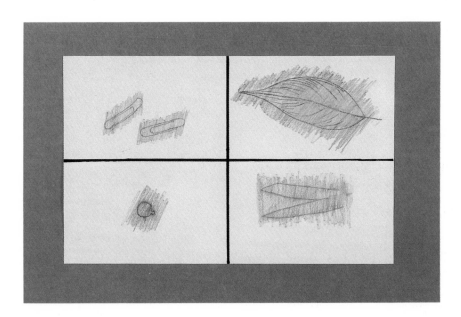

Making Art

1. Look at the textures shown by the rubbings in this lesson. Think of other things with textures. Choose four small things from which you can make rubbings.

2. Place one textured item on a flat place. Lay a piece of thin paper over it. Now practice making a rubbing. Turn a soft pencil or crayon on its side. Rub it smoothly across the paper where the object is. Don't press too hard. Try to keep your rubbing motion even. Make your rubbing strokes all the same length. When you complete one rubbing, move the paper to try another.

3. When you have enough practice, plan your final rubbing. Divide a sheet of paper into four sections. Lay one of your textured items under each section. Make a rubbing of each item. Remember to use smooth, even strokes.

4. When the rubbings are done, compare them to the things they show. Do your rubbings show textures? Are any parts of your rubbings not clear? Share the rubbings with a classmate. Can he or she guess the objects you used?

Art Materials
Textured things
Paper
Pencil or crayon

6 *Feeling with Your Eyes*

Looking and Thinking

Sometimes artists create art by joining together interesting things. This kind of art is called **collage**.

Alice Parrott, La Mesa, 1976, Tapestry. Collection of Paul M. Cook, Atherton.

One thing that makes this fabric collage interesting is the way it uses textures. What kinds of textures do you see in the collage? The artwork also has **unity**. Unity means that all the pieces of an artwork look like they belong together. Often an artist will use the same color several times in a picture to create unity. An artist might also use the same **pattern**, or type of design, over and over. This helps create **rhythm**, too. An artwork has rhythm when you can guess where the artist would use colors or shapes again. You can see a certain pattern. Does this collage use the same pattern or color more than once?

This collage was made by a student your age. Does it use the same fabrics and colors over and over?

Making Art

1. You can make collages from many different things. You can use scraps of cloth or other kinds of scraps such as pieces of newspaper, wallpaper, or tissue paper. You can join together things from nature (leaves, bark, grass, etc.) or things from around the house (macaroni, pieces of wire, etc.) For this lesson you will make a fabric collage.

2. Lay out your fabric pieces on a heavy sheet of paper. Move the pieces around until you like the way they look. You can make some pieces **overlap**, or cover up, parts of other pieces. Also, try to use the same colors and patterns more than once. These things will help give your collage unity.

3. Once you have a collage you like, begin gluing. Begin with the pieces that go behind other pieces. You should glue only one piece at a time. Continue gluing until all the pieces are in place.

4. Allow your collage to dry. Then run your hands over it. Do you feel the many textures? Show a classmate where you used colors and patterns more than once.

Art Materials   THINK SAFETY

Fabric scraps

Paper

Scissors

Glue

---

7 *Shapes Fit Together*

Looking and Thinking

Look at the box on the next page. What do you see in it? Can you see these **shapes** in the world around you? A shape is formed when lines meet and enclose space. Shapes are flat. Trace with your finger the lines of the shapes.

Now look at the two artworks on this page. With a classmate, find as many different shapes as you can in the two pictures. Do you notice any shapes that are used more than once? Are any colors used over and over? Name all the shapes you can find.

Wassily Kandinsky, Open Green, 1923, Oil on canvas, 38¼" x 38¼". The Norton Simon Foundation.

Piet Mondrian, Composition, V., 1914, Oil on canvas, 21⅝" × 33⅝". The Sidney and Harriett Janis Collection, Gift to The Museum of Modern Art, New York.

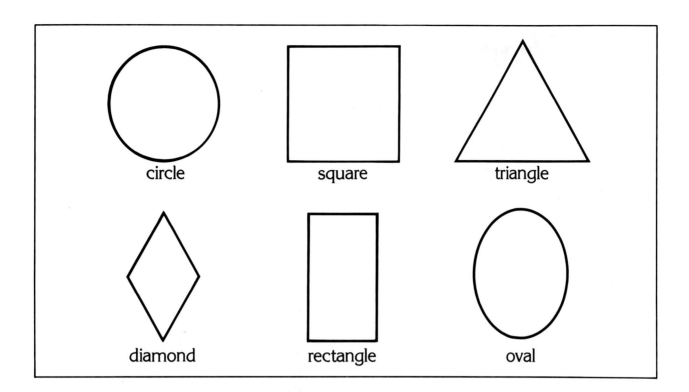

circle   square   triangle

diamond   rectangle   oval

Making Art

1. You can create art out of shapes. First, take chalk and practice drawing the different shapes. See which shapes fit together side-by-side. Try drawing two shapes next to each other so that they share a line. Fill up a sheet of paper with your practice drawings.

2. Now take out a clean sheet of paper. Begin carefully filling it in with shapes. Use a piece of chalk. Make all your shapes fit together. Do not leave any blank spaces. Think about unity. Use some shapes over and over.

3. Once your page is full, begin filling in your shapes with chalk. If you are right-handed, begin filling in the shapes from left to right. If you are left-handed, work right to left. This

will keep your hand from smearing the chalk.

4. Use different colors to fill in your spaces. Think about giving unity to your design by using the same colors over and over.

5. Study your design when it's completed. Did you use the same shapes several times? Did you use the same colors over and over? Would you say your picture has unity?

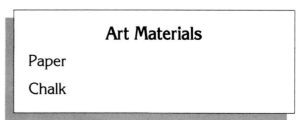

Art Materials

Paper

Chalk

8 Seeing Forms in Buildings

Looking and Thinking

Study the objects in the box below. What are they like?
Are the shapes you learned about in the last lesson
found in these objects? When shapes are joined
together so that they enclose space, solid objects
like these are made. These objects are not flat. They
have **form**.

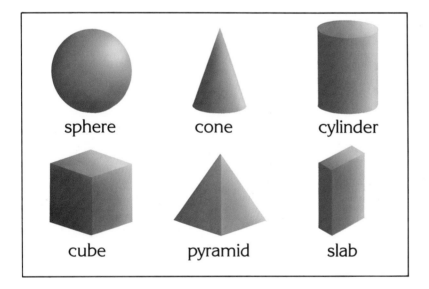

sphere   cone   cylinder

cube   pyramid   slab

You can look at objects with form and learn three
things about them. You can see how tall they are, how
wide they are, and how thick they are from front to
back. Because you can learn these three things from
them, objects with form are called **three-dimensional**.

Objects with form are all around you. Think about
objects you can see from many sides. Find some of
these in your desk. Also think about things you can
walk around. For example, look at the picture on the
next page. Are some of the forms from the box part of
the buildings? Now look at the building created by a
student your age. How many forms do you see?

Making Art

1. Think about things you use every day and then throw away. Boxes, milk cartons, paper cups, and bottle caps are a few things. What other things can you name? Think about the forms of these things. How could you use them to create a model building?

2. Collect the things you will use to make your model. Begin placing them where you think they should go. You will want to work with the big objects first. They should be used for the main parts of your model. Tape or glue them together so they stand up easily.

3. Now add the small objects such as windows, chimneys, and pointed roofs to your building. Tape or glue them firmly in place.

4. You may wish to **decorate** your model more. You can color or paint it or add more details.

5. Share your model with a classmate. See if he or she can find all the shapes and forms you used.

Art Materials

Objects with interesting forms

Scissors, tape, glue, etc.

Paints, crayons, markers, etc.

9 The Highs and Lows of Printing

Looking and Thinking

Do you know what a fingerprint is? A fingerprint is made when the tip of a finger touches a surface and leaves an oily mark. This mark is an exact copy of the ridges of the fingertip. You have probably seen a television show or a movie in which the police search for fingerprints.

Artists make **prints** of different things just like you make fingerprints. Prints are made when the surface of the object making the print is covered with ink or paint. When the object is pressed against the paper, the high parts, which are covered with ink or paint, make a print. The low parts do not have paint or ink on them and do not print. How do you think the objects used to make the prints below would look?

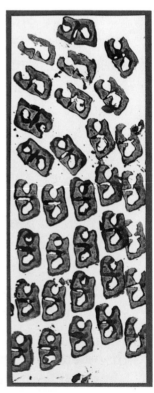

Making Art

1. An easy thing to print with is clay. You can make raised areas on a piece of clay by pressing objects into it. These objects will leave dents in the clay. The dents will not show when the print is made, but the other raised areas will.

2. First take a piece of clay and work it into a cube. Next choose some objects to press into the clay. Choose simple objects that will make deep dents in the clay. Press them firmly into one side of your cube. Then carefully remove the objects. Are the dents deep enough?

3. Put paint on the printing side of your cube. You may brush it on or press your cube against a sponge filled with paint.

4. Press your cube onto paper. Don't press too hard, or you will flatten the cube. Does the print look like you thought it would? Can you see that the raised parts make the print?

5. Fill up a page with your prints. You might want to make them all in a row. Or you might choose to spread them around the page. Just try to make each print in your design clear.

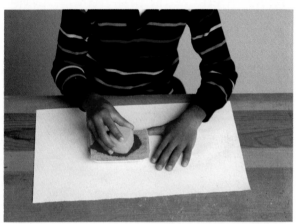

Art Materials

Clay

Paint

Sponge or paintbrush

Paper

Objects

10 Seeing Colors in the World

Looking and Thinking

Have you ever thought about what a colorful world you live in? Look around you. What colors catch your eye? Can you see your favorite color somewhere? Suppose the world suddenly became black-and-white. Think of all the colorful things you'd never see again—sunsets, rainbows, spring flowers.

In the next few lessons, you will learn about colors. You will learn the different kinds of colors. You will also learn how to mix colors. You will use colors to create art.

The colors shown below—red, yellow, and blue—are the **primary colors**. These three colors are important because we can mix them together to make most of the other colors.

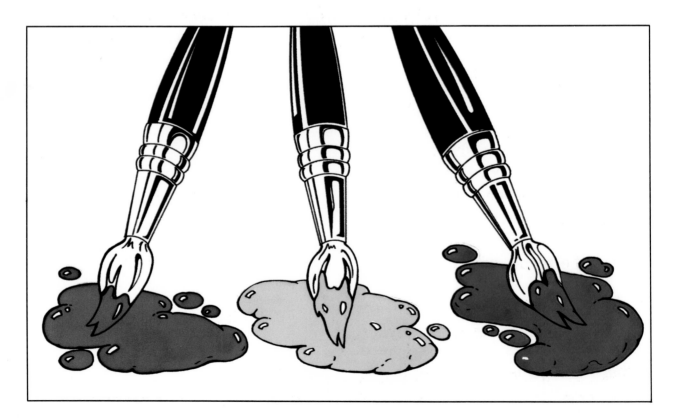

Can you find the primary colors in this colorful painting?

Vasily Kandinsky, Painting No. 201, 1914, Oil on canvas, 64¼" x 48¼." Collection, The Museum of Modern Art, New York, Nelson A. Rockefeller Fund.

Making Art

1. Place a sheet of waxed paper on your desk or table. Work on the waxed paper as you do this lesson.

2. Use tissue paper in the three primary colors. (Can you name these colors?) Cut or tear the tissue paper into interesting shapes. Lay about half of the shapes on the waxed paper. Move them around until you like the way the colors and shapes look.

3. Paint the shapes with starch.

4. Lay the rest of the shapes on top. Overlap them in interesting ways.

5. Paint the whole design with starch. Let it dry.

6. Hold the design up to a light. Can you see the primary colors? What happened when two primary colors overlapped? Was a new color made? Name the new colors that you made.

Art Materials
Waxed paper
Tissue paper (red, yellow, blue)
Liquid starch
Brush

11 More Colors in the World

Looking and Thinking

What do you notice about the pictures in this lesson? What would you say about them if you were telling a friend about them?

One thing you could talk about is how colorful the pictures are. How many different colors do you see? Find the primary colors first. Then see if the pictures use the other three colors shown on the **color wheel** below. These other colors are called **secondary colors**. They are made when two primary colors are mixed.

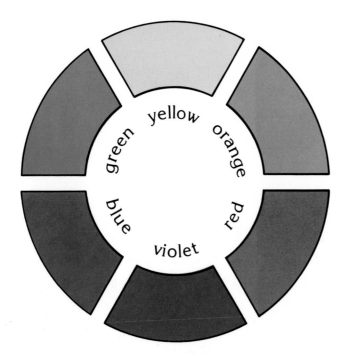

Look closely at the color wheel. Find the primary colors. Notice that violet is in between red and blue. This means that violet is made when red and blue are mixed. What two colors make orange? What two colors make green? Can you think of any other colors the color wheel doesn't show? Where on the color wheel do you think these colors would go?

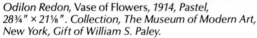
Odilon Redon, Vase of Flowers, *1914, Pastel, 28¾" × 21⅛". Collection, The Museum of Modern Art, New York, Gift of William S. Paley.*

Making Art

1. Think of the most colorful thing you've ever seen. Choose crayons that have the colors you remember the scene or object having. You are going to make a crayon drawing of it.

2. Plan your crayon drawing. Decide where each color should be used. Use the crayons in many ways. You can draw lines with the tips of the crayons. You can lay a crayon on its side to fill in shapes. You can press down hard on a crayon to make a color darker. Just be sure your drawing is colorful.

3. When your drawing is done, give it a name, or **title**. Then, on another piece of paper, write about the colorful thing and where you saw it.

Art Materials
Paper
Crayons

12 Seeing Light in the World

Looking and Thinking

What kind of weather do you think the picture below shows? The men are dressed warmly, but the picture is full of light. Do you like this kind of weather? In which month does it usually occur?

George Caleb Bingham, Fur Traders Descending the Missouri, *Oil on canvas, 29¼" × 36¼". The Metropolitan Museum of Art, Morris K. Jesup Fund, 1933. 33.61*

Paintings like this one are meant to show light. One good way to show light is to use a lot of white and water when painting. You can add white to colors to create **tints**. Notice how the trees in the painting really are not green. The artist mixed a lot of white with his green paint. He created a green tint. What other tints do you see?

Making Art

1. The pictures on this page show how to mix tints. Practice mixing tints. First make a small amount of white paint. Also make a small amount of a color. Drop by drop, add color to the white. After each drop, mix the paints together. Keep adding drops of color until you have the tint you want. Take a small amount of the paint on your brush. Don't use too much. Use your brush to spread a smooth line of paint across a sheet of paper. Do you like the tint you've created?

2. After you have practiced on your own, your teacher will divide the class into small groups. Each group will be given a color. This color will be the one the group uses to make different tints.

3. Each member of the group should work on creating his or her own tint from the color given. Create a tint that you really like. Then paint an index card with your tint.

4. Once all the cards made by your group have dried, spread out the cards. Work as a group to put them in a row. Order them from the one with the most white to the one with the most color. By doing this you are arranging the cards by **value**, from lightest to darkest.

5. When you have the cards in the right order, use tape on the backs to join the row together. Then join your row to all the other groups' rows. Arrange the rows so the colors look nice together. Hang up your rainbow.

Art Materials
Paints
Paper
Brush
Index cards
Tape

13 Colors Can Be Dark

Looking and Thinking

Have you ever been outside really early in the morning? If so, perhaps you've seen the sunrise. Maybe you've been outside on a dark night. Then you could see the moonrise. The picture below is a **photograph** of the moon rising. A man named Edward Steichen used a camera to take the picture. He was a **photographer**. He used paint to make his photograph better. He saw this moonrise somewhere in New York. Does this moonrise remind you of one you've seen?

Edward Steichen, Moonrise— Mamaroneck, New York, *1904, Platinum, cyanotype, and ferroprussiate print, 15¹⁵/₁₆" x 19". Collection, The Museum of Modern Art, New York, Gift of the photographer.*

The picture on the next page was painted by El Greco. He was a famous Spanish painter who lived some 400 years ago. What's happening in the painting? Would you like to be there?

Both of the pictures in this lesson are dark. Black and other dark colors have been added to the colors to make **shades**.

El Greco, View of Toledo, *Oil on canvas, 47¾" × 42¾". The Metropolitan Museum of Art, Bequest of Mrs. H. O. Havemeyer, 1929, The H. O. Havemeyer Collection, 29.100.6*

Making Art

1. Think about how the sky looks just before a storm. What color is it? You can try making that color.

2. Make a small amount of blue paint. Also make some black paint. Add tiny amounts of black paint, drop by drop, to the blue paint. Mix the paints together after each drop. Stop adding black when you think you have made the shade that looks like a stormy sky.

3. Use your paintbrush to cover a piece of drawing paper with the shade you have created. Keep your drawing paper on newspaper so you can cover even the edges. Use smooth strokes and a small amount of paint.

Does your paint look like a stormy sky you've seen?

4. Now use only black paint to make your sky look more like a storm. Paint in swirls of black that look like clouds. Paint in black lines that look like trees. What else should you add to your stormy sky? Use your imagination to finish your stormy sky.

Art Materials

Heavy drawing paper

Paints   Paintbrush

14 Art of the Orient

Looking and Thinking

People who live in hot places have always waved things in the air to create breezes. First, large leaves were used. Then large feathers were used. Finally, around 1,300 years ago, people in Japan invented folding fans. You are going to make a Japanese folding fan for this lesson.

Japan and China are located in the part of the world called the Far East. Art created in the Far East is called **Oriental art**. The artworks below are Oriental art. What kinds of colors were used to make the robe and the bowl? Flowers, dragons, and butterflies are often found in Oriental art. Can you find these things on the robe and bowl?

Early Edo Period, Deep Bowl with Lid, Late 17th century, Porcelain painted in underglaze blue and overglaze enamels, Arita ware, Kakiemon type, 13¾" × 12⅜". The Metropolitan Museum of Art, The Harry G. C. Packard Collection of Asian Art, Gift of Harry G. C. Packard and Purchase, Fletcher Rogers, Harris Brisbane Dick and Louis V. Bell Funds, Joseph Pulitzer Bequest and The Annenberg Fund, Inc. Gift, 1975.

Tibetan Period, Coat (chuba), for Lay Artistocrat, 17th - 18th century, Silk, wrapped gold on cream silk, wrapped peacock feather filaments on silk thread, 62" × 75". The Metropolitan Museum of Art, Rogers Fund, 1962. 62.206

Making Art

1. From your teacher get a piece of paper. You can fold this paper like a fan. Begin on the right side. Make all your folds one finger wide. First fold the right side over to the left. Make a crease. Now fold it backwards so it goes under the fan and to the left. Make the fold exactly as wide as the first one. Make a crease. Now fold it up and to the left again. Keep folding up and then back until you have folded the whole paper.

2. Open the fan. Use a pencil to draw designs on it. You may want to use the designs of Oriental art, such as dragons, butterflies, and flowers. You don't need to cover the whole fan.

3. When you like the way your designs look, decide what colors to use. Remember that Oriental art has lots of primary colors. Choose felt-tip markers in the colors you think best. Use them to color your design.

4. When your fan is complete, staple all the folds together at the bottom. Can you feel a breeze when you wave your fan?

Art Materials

Heavy white paper

Pencil

Felt-tip markers

Stapler

15 Seeing Near and Far

Looking and Thinking

What do you see when you look out your classroom or bedroom window? Do you see trees? Can you see buildings? Think about what you see. How can you tell that things are far away? How are these things different from those that are close?

Study the picture below. Which stairs are closest? How can you tell? Are all the stairs the same?

The stairs in the picture *are* all the same. The ones that are far away look smaller. You can also see less of the stairs that are farther away. This is because the closer stairs **overlap**, or cover up, parts of the farther stairs. You notice these two things when you look at objects that are near and far. These are clues that give you **perspective**. Perspective is a word that means showing distance by giving seeing clues.

Do you know what kind of animal this colorful picture shows? These animals are *buffalo.* Notice how the artist overlapped his buffalo. What else could the artist have done to help show which buffalo are near and which are far?

Creative Director: Primo Angeli; Designers: Primo Angeli, John Gaccione, Tandy Belew.

Making Art

1. In the box are simple animal shapes. Can you name the animals? Now try drawing the shape of an animal you like. Go slowly, and make your lines simple.

2. Your teacher will give you pieces of construction paper in three sizes. From the sheets, cut out your animal shapes. Make each animal as big as the sheet of paper.

3. Lay out the large piece of butcher paper your teacher gives you. Then place your colorful animal shapes on the paper. Arrange them in rows that show distance. Remember the two clues that help show perspective. Be careful to place the shapes by size and to overlap them.

4. Once you're sure your shapes are in the right places, begin gluing them to the paper. Start at the back of each row and work toward the front.

5. Give your picture a title. Then share your picture with others. Can they tell that it shows distance?

Art Materials	
Pencil	
Drawing paper	
Colored construction paper	
Scissors	
Butcher paper	
Glue	

Exploring Art

Art Careers

In this unit you have learned about the elements of art. You have looked at many pieces of art. You have begun seeing art all around you. All of these things are important to you as an artist and as an observer of the world. These things will also be important to you if you choose an art career.

There are many kinds of artists who make many kinds of art. One interesting art career is billboard painting. Usually the design a billboard artist is given is just drawn on a piece of paper. The artist has to make this small design big enough for the billboard. To do this, he or she uses a **grid**. A grid is a piece of paper divided into squares of equal size. The whole grid stands for the billboard. Each square on the grid stands for a square in the same place on the billboard. First, the billboard artist draws the design on the grid. Then the part of the design in each square of the grid is made bigger in the right square on the sign. It is interesting work. It's like putting the pieces of a puzzle together. Each little piece is completed as its own design. Yet all the pieces fit together to make the big design.

Think of other kinds of interesting work that artists do. Find out about one art career that you especially like. Write a report about this career. Share what you learn with your class. Have a special Art Careers Day.

Review

Looking at Art

Stuart Davis, New York Elevated. *San Diego Museum of Art Collection.*

1. What kinds of lines do you see in the painting? Do any of the lines combine to make shapes?

2. Can you find any forms in the painting?

3. Does the painting have primary colors? Does it have secondary colors? Can you find tints or shades in the painting?

4. Does the painting show texture very well?

5. Does the painting show perspective? How?

6. Does the painting have a center of interest? If so, what is it?

7. What do you like best about this painting?

Unit 2

Working as an Artist

As you learn more and more about art, you can begin seeing more and more in the world. For example, look at the photographs on this page. What do you see? Look at the pictures as an artist.

In the picture on the left, you can see shapes, forms, texture, and balance. What else can you see?

In the picture on the right, you can see lines, colors, texture, and rhythm. What else can you see?

Use your magic square to help you see more. Move it slowly across the photographs.

Eastman Johnson, The Brown Family, 1869, Paper, mounted on canvas, 23⅜" x 28½." National Gallery of Art, Washington, Gift of David Edward Finley and Margaret Eustis Finley.

As you learn to see more as an artist, you also learn how to show what you know. You will not always show what you see. Sometimes you will show what you feel. Sometimes you will just show one or two of the elements of art.

Do you think the artist of this painting was good at showing what he saw? What details of the painting do you like best? How did the artist show texture? How did he show perspective? Study the shadows in the painting. What do they help to show? As you continue working as an artist, you too will learn some tricks that will make your pictures show the things you want them to show.

16 Seeing Background and Foreground

Looking and Thinking

Study the picture below. What do you see? Can you see trees and a sailboat? Can you tell where land meets water? Do you see where the sky meets the earth? It's not easy, is it?

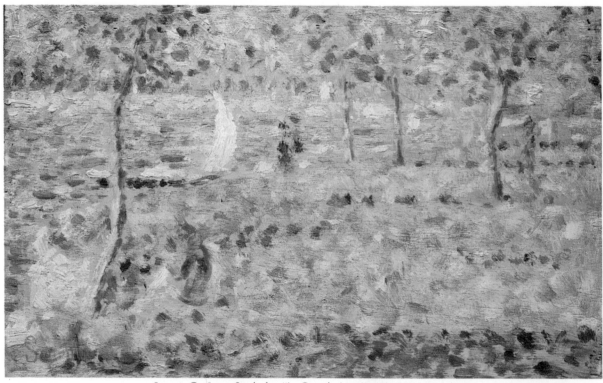

Seurat, Georges, Study for "La Grande Jatte", 1884/1885, Wood, 6¼" x 9⅞", National Gallery of Art, Washington, Ailsa Mellon Bruce Collection.

The paintings in this lesson do not have clear backgrounds and foregrounds. The **background** of a landscape painting is the part that is far away. (A **landscape** painting is a painting of an outdoor scene.) What should be the background of the painting above? The **foreground** of a painting is made up of the things that are near. These are usually the things you notice most.

Study this picture. Can you tell what it is? The title of the picture tells us it shows the sun and the moon. Can you see them? It's hard to see the different parts, isn't it?

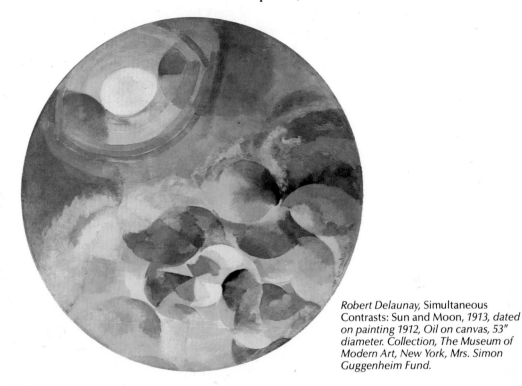

Robert Delaunay, Simultaneous Contrasts: Sun and Moon, *1913, dated on painting 1912, Oil on canvas, 53" diameter. Collection, The Museum of Modern Art, New York, Mrs. Simon Guggenheim Fund.*

Making Art

1. For this lesson you are going to create a colorful background out of blobs of paint. For the next lesson, you will do the foreground.

2. First, make three or four colors of paint. You want to choose light colors. Remember that you can create light colors, or tints, by starting with white.

3. Work on newspaper. Take a large amount of paint on your brush. Spread it evenly across a small part of a heavy sheet of white paper. Use enough paint so that it looks wet and stands in small puddles. Use each color on a small part of the page, until the page is full.

4. Place a piece of heavy white paper over your painted page. Use your hands to smoothly rub this paper. Make it touch the whole painted page. Now peel off the top paper. Did all your colors blend together on this paper?

5. What kind of background could your blended colors be? Can you see sky, grass, or bodies of water in it?

Art Materials
Paints
Brush
Heavy white paper

17 Seeing with Your Mind's Eye

Looking and Thinking

Have you been outside on a foggy morning? What did things look like? Could the picture below be of a foggy morning? This picture was painted in the style called **Impressionism**. Impressionists knew that light is really made of many colors. To show light, they used many spots of color. Can you see spots of color in this painting?

Claude Monet, Cliffs of Pourville, Morning, 1897, Oil on canvas, 25" x 38⅗." The J. Paul Getty Museum. 56. PA. 4

The painter of this picture is Claude Monet. He was a famous Impressionist. Notice how hard it is to tell the background from the foreground in his painting. This is true of many Impressionist paintings.

Study this black-and-white drawing. This picture is very different from an Impressionist painting. Can you name some differences? Does the picture have a clear background? Can you see exactly where the sky meets the ground? How do you think colors would change the picture?

Fra Bartolommeo, Hermitage on a Slope, Drawing, 16th century, 11 7/16" x 8 1/2". Courtesy of the Art Institute of Chicago, The Clarence Buckingham Collection. 57.530

Making Art

1. Look closely at the colorful blobs you created for the last lesson. Think about how you could use them as background. Can you see sky, land, bodies of water, or clouds? Use your imagination. How could you add to the blobs to make a picture? What kind of ink drawing would fit into the background? Think of simple objects to add to the blobs as foreground. Choose ideas that will use very few lines. Try using a black pen with a broad tip to draw the objects on a practice sheet of paper. Use as few lines as you can.

2. Now draw the objects right on your colorful blobs. Use the blobs as background, and draw the objects where you think they should go.

3. When you've added all your foreground objects, study your artwork. How could you make it better? Maybe you should draw lines where the different parts of the background meet. Perhaps your picture is already clear enough. Ask a friend what he or she thinks.

Art Materials

Drawing paper

Colorful blobs from last lesson

Black ink pen

18 *Art Can Fly!*

Looking and Thinking

In almost all parts of the world, boys and girls fly kites. In Japan there is a holiday called Boys Day when many people fly kites. Kites that look like fish are flown from tall poles on the houses. There is one fish kite for every boy in the house. (If there are five kites, how many boys live in the house?) Teams of boys and men fly large kites. There are even kite fights. Have you ever flown a kite?

Today you will make a kite of your own. You will use crayons and paint together. You can hang the kite up in your room. Your teacher might also help you make the kite ready to fly. Either way, your kite will be colorful and fun.

This kite was made by a student artist just like you. What do you like best about it?

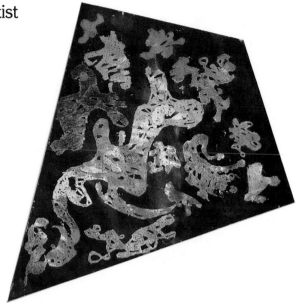

Making Art

1. Lightly draw your design on the kite paper. Use a pencil. Think about the shape of your kite as you draw the design. Do they go together?

2. Think about the colors you want your kite to have. What light, bright colors of crayons will you use?

3. Color your design using the colors you choose. Press hard with the crayons so that there is a lot of wax on your paper. Leave some areas that are not covered with crayon.

4. Now choose the color of paint you will use. It cannot be the same color as any of the crayons. It should be a dark color. Use a lot of water when you make the paint.

5. Put your kite on top of newspapers. Paint over the whole kite paper. Pull the brush only one way. Do *not* scrub back and forth over the same place. This will make the paint too thick over the wax. Watch what happens as the kite dries. Do the paint and crayons mix?

6. Add a tail to your kite. Use string or ribbon and bright shapes of construction paper.

Art Materials

White paper for kite

Pencil

Crayons

Paint

Brush

String or ribbon

Scissors

Construction paper

19 *Does Your World Have Only One Color?*

Looking and Thinking

Have you ever been in a place that seemed to be all one color? Maybe it was your best friend's purple bedroom. It could have been the red lobby of a movie theater. Perhaps you've been outside on a beautiful day when the whole world seemed blue.

The artists of the pictures in this lesson are showing us a blue world. In fact, the picture below is really a photograph. The artist used a camera to make the picture. He took this picture in Germany.

What part of the picture is not blue? Would you like to visit this place?

Pictures that use mostly one color have a long name: **monochromatic**. Can you think of other pictures you could make using only blue? What pictures could you make using only yellow or only green?

This picture is a painting. Is it all blue? What parts are not blue?

Edward Hopper, The Long Leg, *1935, 20" x 30". The Huntington Library, Art Collections, Botanical Gardens.*

Making Art

1. Close your eyes and think of blue things. A field of flowers, your little brother's eyes, a lake, the sky. . . . Keep thinking until you remember something really blue.

2. Use a piece of chalk to make a sketch of your blue idea. Make your idea fill the page. Think about how many different kinds of blue paint you'll need. First make some pure blue. Then mix some tints and shades of blue. Do you remember how? Lessons 12 and 13 can help you.

3. Begin painting your picture. Use a small amount of paint and apply it with smooth strokes. Try to make your blues **blend** together. Don't just stop using one blue and start using another. Instead, make your blues overlap. Leave blank the parts of your picture that aren't blue.

4. When you're done with your blues, study your painting. Could you better blend some of the blues? Do you like the way the blank, white parts look?

5. When your painting is finished, share it with a classmate. Tell where and when you saw the blue scene. Tell how it made you feel.

Art Materials

Chalk

Paper

Paints

Brush

20 *Do You Feel Warm or Cool?*

Looking and Thinking

Study the two pictures in this lesson. How are they alike? How are they different? How does each painting make you feel? How do you think the people in each painting feel? Why do you suppose you think these things about the artworks?

Did you notice how different the colors of the two paintings are? This has something to do with how they make you feel. What colors are used in the picture below? It is mostly blue. Blue is called a **cool color**.

Now look at the picture on the next page. It is painted with **warm colors**. Does the painting make you feel warm?

Turn to the color wheel on page 22. Decide which colors are warm and which are cool. For help, think about how the colors make you feel.

Henry Moore, Figures in a Setting. *The Phillips Collection, Washington, D.C.*

44

Jean-Honoré Fragonard, The Visit to the Nursery, *before 1784, Canvas, 28¾" x 36¼". National Gallery of Art, Washington, Samuel H. Kress Collection.*

Making Art

1. How do you feel today? Are you feeling "cool"? Are you sad or tired, calm or quiet? Or are you feeling "warm"? Do you feel happy or excited, loud or wild? Think about how you feel, about your **mood.**

2. Choose a color that matches your mood. Paint a sheet of paper with this color.

3. On a separate sheet of paper, draw yourself. Make it a simple drawing. It should show the way you feel. You may want to show just your face. Use a pencil or pen. You don't need to color it. Cut out the picture and glue it to your painted paper.

4. Write a story that tells about your picture. Tell what kind of day you are having. Tell about your mood. Copy your story onto a piece of paper. Glue it to the back of your picture. Write the date beneath it. Now you can always remember how you felt today!

Art Materials	THINK SAFETY
Paper	Glue
Paint	Scissors
Brush	Pencil or pen

21 *What Is Cloth Made Of?*

Looking and Thinking

Your clothes are made of cloth, or **fabrics**. Do you know what fabrics are made of? Have you ever had a rip in the knee of your pants? What did it look like? Could you see threads in the rip? Threads are what make up fabrics. Many threads are **woven** together to create cloth.

Cloth weaving is done by taking threads over and under other threads. Other types of weaving can be done with other materials. For this lesson you will make a weaving out of paper strips.

The picture below is of a plan for a weaving. The artist wanted to see how her weaving would look before she began it. Can you see how the parts will be worked over and under each other?

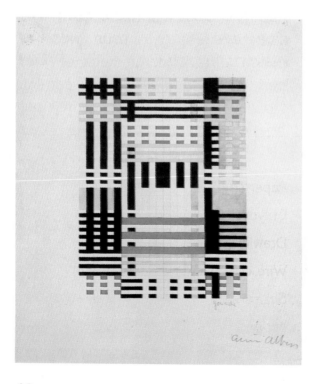

Anni Albers, Preliminary Design for Wall Hanging, *1926, Gouache on paper, 14" × 11½". Collection, The Museum of Modern Art, New York, Gift of designer.*

Making Art

1. Choose strips of paper in four colors that look good together. You will need 24 strips.

2. Make a plan for a weaving. Use crayons in the four colors you have chosen. Make lines up and down and across to show the parts of your weaving.

3. Sort the paper strips into two piles of twelve. Set one pile aside. Fold one end of each of the other twelve strips. Make the fold two fingers wide. Place the fold over the bottom wire of a coat hanger. Put tape where the fold reaches around the wire to the back of the strip. Follow your plan as you put the strips on the wire. When all twelve strips of paper are hanging from the coat hanger, move them so they are together in the center of the wire. These strips are the **warp** of your weaving.

4. Hang your coat hanger up so that you can easily reach it. Begin weaving a strip of paper through the hanging strips. Take it *under* the first strip and *over* the next strip. Work under and over all twelve hanging strips. Now push your **weft** (the strip you have woven through) up as far as it will go. Then fold the two ends back and tape them in place.

5. Weave the remaining strips in the same way. Remember to follow your plan. Be sure if one strip begins *over* that the next strip begins *under*.

6. When your weaving is done, cut off what is left of the hanging strips. Turn the ends up in the back and tape them. Does your weaving match your plan?

Art Materials

Paper strips

Crayons

Drawing paper

Wire coat hanger

Scissors

Tape

22 Going 'Round and 'Round

Looking and Thinking

Look at the staircase below. It is called a **spiral** staircase. A spiral is made when a line curves around and around toward a center point. Can you see how the stairs make a spiral?

Think about flower centers, seashells, a coiled snake, and snail shells. All of these have spirals. Have you seen some other spirals in nature?

One famous artist named Vincent van Gogh often saw and painted the spirals in nature. He painted this tree. Can you see spirals in the painting?

Vincent van Gogh, The Mulberry Tree, *1889, Oil on canvas, 21¼" x 25⅝". Norton Simon Art Foundation.*

Making Art

1. Choose three colors of construction paper. Use scissors to cut circles out of the construction paper. Make the circles all different sizes. Cut out ten or twelve circles.

2. Now use scissors to make spirals in the circles. Begin cutting at the outer edge. Cut around and around toward the center.

3. Experiment with the spirals you have made. Pull the center away from the end of one of the spirals. How does it look? Hold the center down and let the spiral pop up. How does this look? Make all different kinds of designs with the spirals.

4. Begin taping your spirals to a piece of cardboard as you experiment with them. Let them dance across the cardboard. Let them pop up and spring across one another. Make sure you tape them well so they won't fall off.

5. Take your creation home. Tell someone about spirals. Point out some spirals in nature.

Art Materials

Colored construction paper

Cardboard

Scissors

Tape

23 *Lines Can Be Joined in Space*

Looking and Thinking

Look closely at the sculpture below. Notice how the sculptor just joined different kinds of lines together in space. How many types of lines do you see?

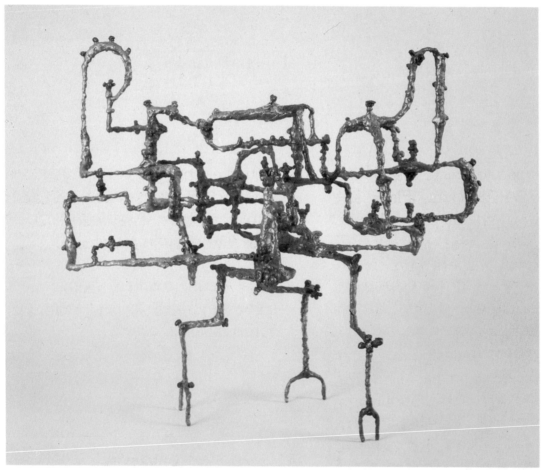

Ibram Lassaw, Corax, 1953. The Peggy Guggenheim Collection of Modern Art, Venice, Italy, Courtesy Fondazione Solomon R. Guggenheim.

Now study the sculpture to see how it stands up. It has legs. It also has the same number of lines on one side as on another. The two sides are **balanced**. The right side is not exactly like the left side. Yet the two sides look enough alike to please the eye.

Do these sculptures, made by students your age, look balanced?

Making Art

1. You are going to create a sculpture out of pipe cleaners. First, just experiment with a pipe cleaner. Notice how it feels and how it bends. Try to shape it in a certain way. Can you do it? Try to shape it in several other ways.

2. Now think of a design for your sculpture. Decide what kinds of lines it will have. Think about how to join the lines together. If you want to, make a pencil drawing of how your sculpture will look. Make sure it looks balanced.

3. Begin joining together your pipe cleaners. Create many kinds of lines out of them. Look at the lines and the shape of your sculpture from different sides. Change it until

you like what you see as you turn your sculpture around. Does your sculpture look balanced? Does it look interesting from all sides?

4. Tape or glue your sculpture to a piece of cardboard, and write your name on it.

Art Materials THINK SAFETY

Pipe cleaners

Pencil

Paper

Glue or tape

Cardboard

24 Right Side, Left Side, or Both?

Looking and Thinking

Draw a heart on a sheet of paper. Cut out the heart. Draw a line down the middle of it. Use a ruler for help. Is the right side just like the left side? Fold your heart along the center line so that the two sides meet. Do the sides match? When one half of a thing is like the other half, the object has **symmetry**.

Many things in nature have symmetry. Most animals do. Some have two eyes, two front legs, and two back legs. Many plants also have symmetry. Can you think of other things in nature that show symmetry?

Does the owl show symmetry?

Does this picture show symmetry?

Do these butterflies show symmetry?

Making Art

1. Fold a piece of paper in half from left to right. Crease the fold. Pretend the fold is the center of a butterfly. Imagine the butterfly as if you were looking down at it. Then use a pencil to draw the right side of the butterfly. Keep the paper folded as you work.

2. First, show the three parts of the butterfly's body. These are the head, the thorax (like your chest), and the main body. Then show the upper and lower wings. Add the antennae. The butterflies above have all these parts. Study them for help.

3. When you're finished with the right half of your butterfly, open the paper. Then draw the left side of your butterfly. Remember to show symmetry. Make the left side look just like the right side.

4. Use a black felt-tip pen to make the lines of your butterfly thick. Then add designs to your butterfly's wings. Color them with bright colors. Use crayons or felt-tip pens. Make sure your designs also show symmetry. Make your butterfly as beautiful and colorful as you can.

Art Materials	
Scissors	
Ruler	
Paper	
Pencil	
Black felt-tip pen	
Crayons or colorful pens	

53

25 Thumbs Up for Art

Looking and Thinking

Do you think the same hand made all the handprints in the poster below? How does each one look different? When things are changed slightly, **variety** is created. Variety makes art interesting.

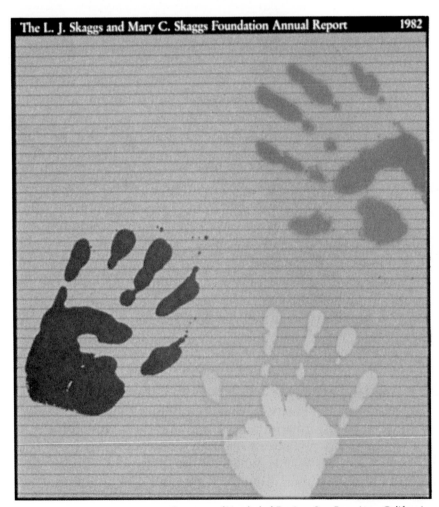

The L. J. Skaggs and Mary C. Skaggs Foundation Annual Report   1982

Courtesy of Vanderbyl Design, San Francisco, California.

This poster was created as a type of **advertisement**. An advertisement tells people about something in order to get them interested in it. Many advertisements are very simple, like this one.

How do the doll heads in this picture look the same? How do they look different? Does this variety make the picture interesting?

Making Art

1. You can create a picture from your own thumbprints. You can make it interesting by using variety. Using several colors will help. Changing the way you hold your thumb will also add variety. You can print with your whole thumb. You can also use the sides, tip, and back of your thumb. You will always use the same thumb, but in different ways. This will create variety.

2. Choose three colors of paint. Make the paint thicker than usual. Pour the colors into three paint trays. Place your thumb in one of the trays. Make thumbprints on a large piece of white paper. Change the way you hold your thumb to make more prints. Make many prints using this color. Then try the next color. Overlap some of the prints. Keep changing the way you hold your thumb. Now try the third color. Put these thumbprints where they look best. Think about rhythm. Do your prints have a certain pattern that you should add to?

3. When your picture is done, count how many different prints you made. Would your picture be as interesting if most of the prints were the same?

Art Materials

Paints

Paint trays

Paper

26 By the Light of the Moon

Looking and Thinking

All through time, people have noticed the full moon.
Some people have said it makes them act strangely.
Others have written spooky stories about it. Many
artists have shown moonlight in their works. The two
paintings in this lesson are examples. Why do you
think the full moon seems so important?

Have you ever been outside on a night with a full
moon? The moon seems to light up the whole sky. It
fills the night with a soft glow. Maybe this is why it
seems so important.

Kawase Hasui, Hinomisaki in Moonlight in Izumo Province. *San Diego Museum of Art, Gift of Mrs. Clark Cavenee.*

How is this painting like the one on the left page?

Ralph Albert Blakelock, Moonlight. *In the collection of The Corcoran Gallery of Art, William A. Clark Collection.*

Making Art

1. You are going to make a picture showing a moonlit night. First, plan the spaces in your picture. Will you show more land or more sky? Decide where in your picture the sky will meet the ground. This is the **horizon**. With a pencil draw your horizon line across a sheet of paper.

2. Now think about the moon. What color do you think it is? Make some paint of this color. On your paper, paint a round, full moon in the center of the sky.

3. Add black to your paint until you create the **shade** that reminds you of moonlight. Use this shade to paint the sky. Start in the center, around your moon. Work out, toward the edges of your paper. As you get farther and farther from the moon, add more and more black. Fill the whole sky.

4. Paint the land part of your picture solid black.

5. Decide where your moonlit scene is. What things should stand out against the moonlit sky? Cut the shapes of these things out of black construction paper.

6. Wait until your painting is dry. Then glue your shapes to it. Make up a name for the place your painting shows. This can be the title. Does your picture show the special magic of the moon?

Art Materials THINK SAFETY

Paper	Black construction paper
Pencil	
Paint	Scissors
Brushes	Glue

27 Let's Get to the Important Part

Looking and Thinking

Study the photograph below. Can you tell what parts of the scene are in front of other parts? Can you tell what is near and what is far? Do you remember the big word that tells about these things?

The photograph above shows a lot of small parts, or details, of the scene. What are some of these details? The picture also shows one very important thing. It was probably the first thing you saw when you looked at the picture. What is it? This part of the picture is called the **center of interest**. It is the most important part of the scene.

What is the center of interest in this painting? One clue is to look where the people in the painting are looking.

Georges Seurat, Le Cirque (The Circus), 1890-91, Oil on canvas, 25¼" x 20". Museé du Louvre, Paris.

Making Art

1. Think of a fun place you've been. It could be a park, a zoo, or even your friend's house. But it should be a real place that you've seen. You are going to use crayons to draw this fun place.

2. Think of the most important part of the place. Begin by drawing this part. This will be the center of interest of your artwork.

3. Draw the rest of the place around the center of interest. Use overlapping to show perspective. You should also make things that are far away look smaller than things that are near.

4. Carefully plan how to use the spaces of your picture. Remember that your center of interest is the most important part. It should be big. Don't let any other parts hide it. If you show people, you might want them to look at your center of interest.

5. See if a classmate can guess your center of interest.

Art Materials
Paper
Crayons

28 Animals in Art

Looking and Thinking

Have you ever seen any wild animals? If you've been to the zoo, you have. You also could have seen wild animals on television shows and movies, or in books. Think about some of the wild animals you have seen.

Long ago men who went to war made themselves look like wild animals. They thought this would frighten away other men. Warriors also used to be given animal names that told how brave they were. What animal name would you like?

Italy, Parade Sallet, ca. 1460. The Metropolitan Museum of Art, New York, Harris Brisbane Dick Fund, 1923.

This lion's head was worn 500 years ago by an Italian warrior. Would you like to wear this helmet on your head?

Throughout time, people have liked to show and tell about imaginary animals. One imaginary animal many people like is the unicorn. This piece of art shows a unicorn. What is unusual about the unicorn?

Artist Unknown, Unicorn Tapestry, Sight (detail), *end of 15th century. Museé de Cluny, France.*

Making Art

1. Think of an animal you would like to show. It could be a wild animal or an animal you imagine. Think about how its face and head should look. You are going to make its head by stuffing and decorating a bag.

2. Crumple some newspaper or other scrap paper into small balls. Stuff the balls into a small brown sack. Push as many balls of paper into the sack as you can. You want the sack to be filled so it has form. When the sack is full, tie it closed with string.

3. Now make the sack head look like the animal. You can paint the bag. You can add yarn for hair or buttons for eyes. You can use construction paper for ears or horns. Think about the art materials you know how to use. Choose the ones you need. Remember to make one side of the bag show the face and the other side show the head. Think of a name for your new pet.

Art Materials

Small brown paper sack

Newspaper

String

Scissors

Paint, yarn, construction paper, buttons, etc.

Tape, glue, staples, etc.

---

29 *Give Your Finger a Face*

Looking and Thinking

A *play* is a story acted out by real people. Much work goes into planning a play. People have to be chosen to play the parts, or *roles*. Often clothes have to be made for the people. The clothes have to fit the time and place of the story. The place where the play occurs also has to look like it fits the story. Many times a big piece of cloth or wood will be painted to look the way it should. This is called the *backdrop*.

In the next two lessons your class will get ready to put on its own play. You will make puppets to fill the roles. You will make clothes for your puppets. When you are ready to put on the play, you will create a backdrop for it.

These puppets were made by student artists. In what kind of play could they be used?

Making Art

1. Talk with your classmates about the kind of play you will put on. Decide what roles the play needs. Then decide what kind of puppet each of you should make.

2. Today you will just make the head of your puppet. You will need a balloon blown up to the size of your fist. Cover the balloon with a layer of clear jelly.

3. Dip a strip of paper into the wheat paste your teacher has ready. Get a lot of the paste on your strip. Then put the strip on your balloon. Smooth out the strip. Keep adding strips to your balloon. Cover all of the balloon. Just leave one hole at the bottom of the balloon. It should be as big around as your second finger. Add four or five more layers of strips. Be sure to smooth down each strip.

4. Let the strips dry on your balloon. Then cut out the hole you left. Your teacher will help you. Put your finger through the hole and wriggle it. Does your puppet head move along with your finger?

5. Now paint your puppet head. Remember to make your puppet's face fit its role. Think about the kind of eyes your puppet should have. Think about how your puppet feels—sad, happy, angry. The puppet's face should show this. Use other art materials to add details like hair.

Art Materials

THINK SAFETY

Wheat paste	Balloon
Scissors	Petroleum jelly
Paint	Newspaper

30 Clothes Are Art, Too

Looking and Thinking

Have you ever thought of your clothes as art? Clothes *are* art. You wear colors that go well together. You choose patterns that don't clash with one another. You pick out clothes that look good on you.

Clothes also tell something about how a person lives. They tell if the weather where the person lives is hot or cool. They tell if a person is going to school, to a party, or to the playground. Clothes often tell what kind of work a person does. What do the clothes below tell?

Pende people of Zaire, Raffia costumes of Minganji dancers, *National Museum of African Art. Smithsonian Institution, Eliot Elisofon Archives.*

This outfit was worn by a woman in northern China. What colors and patterns do you see in it?

This outfit is worn for a special ceremony in Africa. It is made of something similar to rope. Would you like to wear this?

64

This statue is of a ballet dancer. Do the clothes help tell this? You can make clothes that help tell about your puppet.

Hilaire Germain Edgar Degas, Little Fourteen-Year-Old Dancer, *executed about 1880-1881; probably cast in 1922, Bronze, tulle skirt and satin hair ribbon, 39". The Metropolitan Museum of Art, Bequest of Mrs. H. O. Havemeyer, 1929, The H. O. Havemeyer Collection. 29.100.370*

Making Art

1. Decide what clothes fit the role of your puppet. How can you make the clothes? What art materials can you use?

2. Cut out the shapes of the clothes. Use paper or fabric. You can make the clothes wrap around your hand as your finger holds the puppet's head. You can also make the clothes just big enough to hide your hand. Decide which way is best.

3. Color the clothes or paint them. Add designs and patterns if you want to. Also add buttons and ruffles and other details. Use real objects or draw them on the clothes. If you draw the details, remember to show textures. Clothes have many different textures. Use your imagination to show the textures.

4. Use tape to attach the clothes to the puppet's head. Hold the puppet on your finger. Ask a classmate if your hand is hidden. Move the puppet with your finger. Do the clothes move, too?

Art Materials

Different kinds of paper

Pieces of fabric

Crayons, paints, markers, etc.

Buttons, ribbons, lace, etc.

Tape   Scissors

Exploring Art

Putting on a Puppet Show

It's time to make the set for your puppet play. As a class, talk about the play you wrote. Decide exactly what kind of backdrop the play needs. Where does the play take place? The backdrop should show this. When does the play take place? The backdrop should show this, too (night or day, hot or cold weather, etc.).

Work together to paint the backdrop. Don't put too many details in it. They will take the attention away from the puppets. Details are also hard to see from far away. Remember that the people watching the play will be several feet away.

Hang up your backdrop. Hang a sheet over a table in front of the backdrop. The sheet will hide the **puppeteers** from the audience. (The puppeteers are the people moving the puppets.)

Practice moving your puppet. Practice saying the puppet's lines. Then join the other puppeteers for a full rehearsal, or practice, of the play.

Put on your puppet play for an audience. When it's over, introduce yourself as the true star behind your puppet!

Review

Creating Art

Jean-Honoré Fragonard, The Visit to the Nursery, before 1784, Canvas,
28¾" x 36¼." National Gallery of Art, Washington, Samuel H. Kress Collection.

1. How did the artist show the moods of the people in this painting?

2. What makes up the background of the painting? What is in the foreground? How did the artist show the difference between the background and the foreground?

3. How did the artist show the center of interest in the painting?

4. Did the artist include any symmetry in the painting?

5. Where does the light come from in this painting? How does the artist show that some things are farther from the light than other things?

6. How many different textures does the painting include? How did the artist show each kind of texture?

7. What do you think the artist did best when making this painting?

Unit 3

The Many Faces of Art

Art has always been where man has been. It has been found in caves where people lived over 40,000 years ago. It has been dug up from cities buried by earthquakes and volcanoes. Ancient artworks remind us of two important things about art. First, they tell us that people use whatever they can to make art. Second, they tell us that busy people cannot always make art just to make art. Instead, they make objects they need and then decorate them. This glass is an example. It is a work of art. But it is also useful.

Artworks have also always been created to tell the world what has happened. This quilt is an example. It was made in honor of Anna Tuells' marriage. Is it also a useful work of art?

Otto Prutscher, Wine goblet, c. 1905, Flashed and hand-painted glass, 8⅛″ high, 3⅛″ diameter at base. Collection, The Museum of Modern Art, New York, Estée and Joseph Lauder Design Fund.

Anna Tuell, Marriage Quilt, 1785, Wadsworth Atheneum.

Art can be useful. Art can celebrate. Art can tell others about what is important. Art lasts as a record of time. What story does the artwork below tell?

In this unit, you will learn many stories from art. You will create art from many things. You will be an international artist.

31 *Art That's Black and White*

Looking and Thinking

Historians are people who study what has happened in the world throughout time. For clues they study things like dishes, tools, buildings, and cities. These things tell how people lived and what they were able to do. Art historians also study what was written and what art was created. These works tell the important things people saw, believed in, and wanted to tell others about.

The oldest art that historians have found was made almost 40,000 years ago. This type of art is called **cave painting**. Most cave paintings showed animals. Often the art was made with a piece of charcoal. Sometimes white, red, and yellow paints were used. Historians believe the cave paintings were meant to tell stories. What story could this cave painting tell?

Courtesy Department Library Services, American Museum of Natural History. Neg. No. 273397

Some artists still use charcoal or pencil to make drawings. Does this picture tell a story about animals?

Doug Lindstrand, from Doug Lindstrand's Alaskan Sketchbook. *Reproduced with permission of Doug Lindstrand, Anchorage, Alaska.*

Making Art

1. Think about an adventure you have had with animals or read about in a story. Think how you could tell in a picture the story of your adventure.

2. Use a piece of black chalk or charcoal to draw your picture. Use your piece of chalk in many ways. Turn it on its side to fill in some of the spaces. Use one corner of it to draw thin lines. The tip can draw thick lines. Keep your drawing simple. Make your lines tell a story. Remember that different lines make you feel different ways. Use lines that tell how your animal felt.

3. Study your drawing. Does the picture tell a story? Share your drawing with a friend. Tell about the animal.

Art Materials

Paper

Black chalk or charcoal

32 Art from Small Pieces

Looking and Thinking

A **mosaic** is an artwork made from many small pieces placed closely together. The artwork below is a mosaic. Can you see the many small pieces? How would the mosaic feel if you touched it?

Paul Horiuchi, Mosaic Mural at the Seattle Center (detail).

Mosaics are usually quite colorful. By using some colors over and over, the artist making a mosaic gives it **unity**. Does the mosaic above have repeated colors? Does it have repeated shapes?

This mosaic was made hundreds of years ago in the country called Syria. Notice how alike the right and left sides of the mosaic are. Pretend there is a line through the middle of the mosaic. See how the two sides **balance**. Each side has a peacock and another animal. What else does each side have? What colors are used throughout the mosaic?

Artist unknown, Vine Rinceau with Two Peacocks, *probably between 526 and 538 A.D., Mosaic, 46" x 150". Worcester Art Museum, Massachusetts. 1936.23*

Making Art

1. To make your own mosaic, cut or tear colorful construction paper into many small pieces.

2. Decide how you want your mosaic to look. Will it show a real-life scene like the mosaic above does? Or will it be a design of shapes like the mosaic on the left page? Sketch the outlines of your mosaic on a piece of heavy white paper. Think about where the different colors will go.

3. Begin gluing your mosaic pieces to the paper. Use a very small amount of glue on the back of each piece. Place your pieces close together. Use some of the same colors throughout your design to give it unity. Fill the page with your mosaic.

4. Run your fingers lightly over the mosaic. How does it feel? Have a classmate stand on the other side of the room and hold up your mosaic. Can you see the small pieces? Do the small pieces go well together to make the whole design?

Art Materials
THINK SAFETY

Colorful construction paper	Heavy white paper
Scissors	Glue
Pencil	

33 Animals Can Be Smooth

Looking and Thinking

Ancient Chinese artists made beautiful sculptures of animals and large vessels (pots and vases) for ceremonies. Shapes for vessels were often animals—snakes, water buffalo, elephants, or dragons. Some of the earliest sculptures that have been found were made of a metal called bronze. These animals were strong and solid looking. Their forms were simple and smooth. In later years the sculptures were richly decorated. These sculptures did not look as powerful. Which sculpture shown in this lesson do you think was made first? Why do you think so?

Chinese, Eastern Han Dynasty, Giant Panda, 25-220 A.D., Gilt bronze, 5⅜". The Saint Louis Art Museum, Museum Purchase.

The Chinese artists were not very interested in carving stone or wood. These materials would not last as long as other, harder materials such as jade. Today you will carve an animal. But you will use soft plaster. It is easier to work with.

Chinese, T'ang Dynasty, Tomb figure: Standing Horse, *618-907 A.D., pottery, 28" x 33." The Metropolitan Museum of Art, Rogers Fund, 1925.*

Making Art

1. Decide what you want to carve out of your plaster block. Think about what the front of it will look like. Think about what the sides will look like. Make quick sketches of your ideas. Then draw the lines right on your plaster block. Show the front, the back, and the sides.

2. Begin cutting away the plaster to your lines. Slowly carve away at the whole block. Turn it as you work. Always carve away from your body.

3. Keep the base, or bottom of your sculpture, whole. This way your sculpture won't fall over. If your sculpture is of something standing, make it have fat legs.

4. Sand or scrape your sculpture smooth.

5. Paint white glue on your sculpture and let it dry.

6. Do you like the form of your sculpture? Does it look solid and sturdy? Would you like to change anything about it?

Art Materials
THINK SAFETY

Plaster block	Sandpaper
Drawing paper	Glue
Pencil	Brush
Table knife	

34 Canadian Indian Art

Looking and Thinking

Before Columbus reached America, the people we now call Indians were the only people on the continent. One tribe of Indians lived in what is now eastern Canada. This was the Micmac tribe. The weather in their part of the world is often cold and snowy. Life for the Micmac Indians was not easy. They had to move about constantly in search of food. They had to make houses, tools, and clothes out of wood and animal skins. Little else could be found.

Even though life was hard for these Indians, they still took time to create art. They made art from things around them. The most famous Micmac art was made by **quilling**. Quilling was done by covering objects with porcupine quills. The Micmac Indians colored the quills with dyes. Then they used the quills to make designs on clothes and objects.

Micmac Indians, Quilled Birch Bark Box. *Museum of the American Indian, Courtesy of Heye Foundation, N.Y.*

This chair cover was made by quilling. What sorts of designs do you see? Do you think this chair cover was made for an important member of the Micmac tribe? Why?

Micmac Indians, Quilled Chair Cover, *1893. Nova Scotia Museum, Halifax.*

Making Art

1. You can use toothpicks to make a quilling design. First, color your toothpicks by placing them in bowls of food coloring or actual dyes. Choose colors that the Micmacs could have used. (Their dyes were made from berries. What berries with color can you name?) Let your toothpicks dry on paper towels or newspapers.

2. Draw a design on the cardboard circle your teacher gives you. Make the design fit the curves of the circle. Keep the shapes of the design large and simple. Your colored toothpicks will fill in the shapes.

3. Use a small amount of glue on each toothpick. Place the toothpicks side by side to fill in the design.

4. Once the design is finished, look closely at it. How might you make it look better? See if someone else can give you ideas for improving your work.

Art Materials

Food coloring or dyes

Cardboard circle

Pencil

Toothpicks

Glue

---

35 American Indian Art

Looking and Thinking

Ancient American Indians named the Mimbres dug clay from the ground. They rolled it into long, thin snake shapes and coiled it and smoothed it to make pottery for everyday use. Their pots had beautiful forms, but they did not have any designs on them. The pots were plain gray.

One hundred years passed. Their pottery began to change. They began to grind up stones of different colors and make paints to decorate their pots. They made animal designs and line designs which were repeated in patterns on their pots. No one knows for sure now just what the designs meant to the Mimbres. We can do what scientists do. We can look at the designs and try to figure out what was important to the Mimbres. Why do you think they painted so many rabbits on their pots? They also painted birds, lizards, and insects. Why?

Rachel Nampeyo, Hopi Jar, 1951. Museum of Northern Arizona Collections.

Today the Hopi Indians still make pots. This pot was made by Hopis. Modern Indian pieces of pottery like this still show animals. Why do you think this is so?

Helen Naha, Hopi Wedding Vase, 1983. Museum of Northern Arizona Collections.

Making Art

1. Create a design that uses Hopi or Mimbres ideas and symbols. Lightly draw your design in pencil on butcher paper. Make the border, or outer edges, a pattern of repeated symbols. You may want to draw an animal in the center. Think about how your design would look on a curved surface. Would curved or straight lines look best? Think about a shape for a piece of pottery. What lines would follow its shape?

2. Go over your design with a fat black marker.

3. Color your design with crayons. Use only three colors. Choose colors that the Indians might use. Press the crayons hard against the paper as you draw.

4. Do your designs and colors look like they would work well on a bowl? Do your curves follow the shape you planned?

Art Materials

Pencil

Butcher paper

Crayons

Black marker

36 Art That Tells Time

Looking and Thinking

Do you know what a calendar is? A calendar shows the days and the months. It is a way of keeping time. Calendars haven't always been as exact as they are now. Around 200 years ago, the Indians in the western part of America began making calendars. These calendars were called *winter counts*. Every winter the leaders of a tribe would get together. They would choose the most important thing that had happened since the last winter. A picture showing this important event would then be drawn on the winter count.

Cheyenne Indians, Buffalo Robe. Courtesy of Museum of the American Indian, Heye Foundation, N.Y.

This is a winter count made by the Cheyenne tribe. Notice that the winter count is drawn on an animal skin. How many drawings do you see on the winter count? Can you tell what the drawings show?

This is a page from a modern calendar. How many things does this page tell? Does the picture tell a story? What does it tell about the weather?

Mary Azarian, December, from A Country Calendar *by Mary Azarian, copyright ©1986 by Mary Azarian. Reprinted by permission of David R. Godine, Publisher, Boston.*

Making Art

1. Tear the edges of a sheet of brown paper. Make the brown paper the size of a piece of drawing paper. Be sure all the edges are torn. Then crumple the brown paper into a loose ball. Open the paper and smooth it out.

2. Paint the brown paper. Use a brush dipped in thin coffee.

3. Let the paper dry. Then use a black marker with a fat tip to make the ragged edges black.

4. Think of the most important thing that happened to you this year. Use the marker to draw a picture of the event. Center the picture on your winter count. Make your drawing simple like the Indians did. Use lines and simple shapes. Remember that lines can tell a story and reveal feelings. Use the right kinds of lines and shapes to tell your story.

5. Share your winter count with your class. Tell about the event it shows.

Art Materials
Brown paper
Coffee
Brush
Black marker

37 *Art to Wear*

Looking and Thinking

A mask hides a person's face. A mask also gives the person a new face. Masks have been important art forms for people of many lands. Some cultures have special ceremonies during which masked people pretend to be gods or spirits. Other cultures use scary masks to frighten away things that are feared. Masks also have been used to show characters in plays.

Today we use masks mostly for fun. Have you worn a mask to a party or on Halloween? Was it fun to be someone or something else?

Peru, Lambayeque, Funerary Mask, 10th - 14th century. Metropolitan Museum of Art, Gift and Bequest of Alice K. Bache.

Mixtec culture, Mexican Highlands (Puebla or Oaxaca), Mosaic Stone Mask of Tlaloc, 1200-1500, Stone with turquoise, shell, and coral inlay. The Saint Louis Art Museum, Gift.

This mask was made more than 700 years ago. Someone in Peru made it to be buried in. It is made from real gold. Notice the shape of the eyes.

This mask was made in Mexico over 500 years ago. It is made from stone. It is decorated with shells and a special blue stone called turquoise.

This mask was made on an island southeast of Alaska. The Haida people lived on the island before 1885. Fishing was important to these people. Does the mask show this?

Kaigani-Haida peoples, Alaska, Mask, 22⅔" x 25¾". Museum of Cultural History, UCLA, Gift of Wellcome Trust.

Making Art

1. You are going to make a mask to cover half your face. The Lone Ranger wore a mask like this. Your teacher will give you a strip of tag board to use.

2. Work with a classmate. Put the strip over your eyes so it touches your forehead and cheeks. Have your classmate carefully touch a marker to the part of the mask where your eyes are.

3. Now take off the strip and cut out the eyes. Push the points of your scissors carefully through the mask to make holes. Work your scissors around to make the holes bigger.

4. Decide the shape you want your eyes to have. (Not all eyes have to be round.) Use your scissors to cut out the eyes. You also might want to change the shape of your strip. Use your scissors to shape it however you want.

5. Now decorate your mask. You can paint it, color it, or put glitter on it. You can hang ribbons or feathers from it. You might want to add things like eyelashes. Use colored paper to do this. Make the mask look however you like.

6. Your teacher will help you add a band to your mask. This will let you wear your mask home to surprise someone.

Art Materials

Strip of tag board

Scissors

Paints, crayons, markers, etc.

Ribbons, feathers, glitter, etc.

Glue

Colored paper

38 Colorful Cloth

Looking and Thinking

Today you will start an art project called **tie-dye**. Tie-dye is a way to make designs in fabrics. People in almost every country in the world know how to tie-dye. Scientists called *anthropologists*, who study the way people live, think tie-dying was first done in China. All the countries that were close to China learned how to tie-dye. Indonesian people make tiny designs in tie-dye. Bright, bold designs are done in Africa. In American cities, you might see people wearing shirts that have been tie-dyed.

To do tie-dye you will tie pieces of string around a piece of cloth. You will also tie things like marbles and nails tightly in the cloth. What do you think will happen when you put that cloth into a pail of brightly colored dye? Today you will find out. The pictures in this lesson should give you hints.

Michi Ouchi, Hanabi (Fireworks), *from* Contemporary Batik and Tie-Dye *by Doña Z. Meilach, 1973, Tie-dyed and discharge dye on cotton, 108" x 46". Reproduced with permission of Crown Publishers, Inc., New York.*

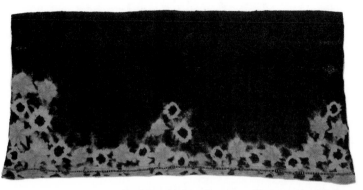

Tunisian tie-dye. *Courtesy of International Gallery, San Diego, California.*

Tunisian tie-dye. *Courtesy of International Gallery, San Diego, California.*

Making Art

1. Decide if you want designs of circles, lines, or both on your cloth. Fold the cloth and tie it with string to make lines. Tie marbles and nails into the cloth to make circles of different sizes. As you work, wind the string tightly around and around the cloth. Tie it tightly.

2. Put your cloth into the soda-soak. Let it stay for 15 minutes. Gently squeeze it to get out the extra water.

3. Put on plastic gloves. Choose the color you want your cloth to be. Put your cloth into the colored dye. Let it stay for 10 minutes.

4. Take the cloth out of the dye. Gently squeeze out the extra dye.

5. Put your cloth into a plastic bag. It needs to stay in the bag for at least two hours.

6. Wash the cloth with soap and water. You should wear the gloves again. Rinse the cloth in cold water. Squeeze it and let it dry.

7. When the cloth is almost dry, put on the gloves one more time. Take the strings off the cloth. Take out the marbles and other things. Take off the gloves. You are finished! Does your fabric have lines and circles? How does it look?

Art Materials

Cloth	Gloves
String	Plastic bag
Marbles, nails, other small objects	Scissors
Soda soak	Soap
Dyebath	

39 Layers and Layers of Crayon

Looking and Thinking

The Aborigines were the first people to live in Australia.
Historians believe the Aborigines reached Australia
over 40,000 years ago. The art made by these people
can be found in caves, on stone, and on pieces of
bark. The Aborigines made paints from berries and
other plants in nature. Then they used the paints to
color imaginative designs.

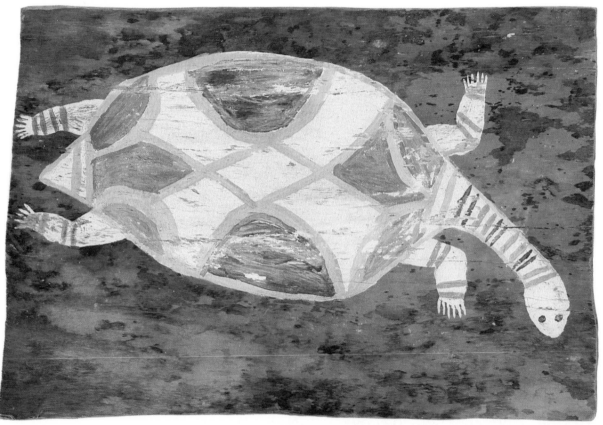

Aboriginal Bark Painting. *Courtesy of San Diego Museum of Man.*

This is an Aboriginal bark painting. It was painted
long ago. What colors does it have? Can you see these
colors in nature? Describe the kinds of shapes and
lines used to make the bark painting.

A student artist like you made this piece of art. Does it remind you of Aboriginal art? The artist used crayons and paper instead of paints and bark. Things like paint, crayons, and clay are called **media**. They are an artist's materials. Can you see how different media change the way art looks?

Making Art

1. Begin your bark painting by covering a sheet of paper with yellow crayon. Use short, quick strokes to cover the paper. Press down on the crayon.

2. On top of the yellow crayon, add a layer using orange crayon. Use quick strokes, and cover the whole page. Don't press down on the crayon quite as hard as you did on the yellow crayon. You don't want to break through the yellow layer.

3. Do three more layers in this order: red, brown, black. (Would the Aborigines be able to use the colors you use?) Then rub the surface of your art with a paper towel.

4. Now use your scissors to **etch** a design in the crayon layers. Use the points of the scissors to etch lines. Use the edges of the scissors to etch out solid areas or shapes. Keep your design simple. Think about how the Aborigines' designs looked.

5. Study your artwork when it's complete. Can you see the colors of crayons where you etched? How is your artwork like an Aboriginal bark painting? How is it different?

Art Materials

White paper

Crayons

Paper towels

Scissors

THINK SAFETY

40 Art That's Life-Sized

Looking and Thinking

Most of the art you have seen in this book is small
enough to hang on the wall or set on a table. Art can
be much bigger. There are beautiful buildings that are
art. There are murals and mosaics a block long. There
are sculptures as tall as ten-story buildings. Have you
seen large art like this?

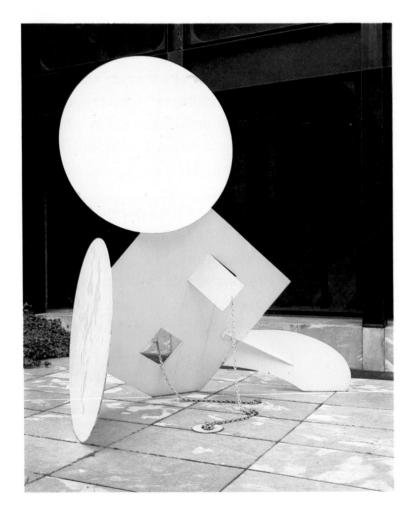

Claes Oldenburg, Geometric
Mouse Scale A, *1975, Painted steel
and aluminum, 12'1½" x 12'6" x
14'10¼". Collection, The Museum
of Modern Art, New York,
Blanchette Rockefeller Fund.*

This piece of art is quite large. It is made of metal.
What does this piece of art show? Find three different
shapes that are part of it.

This large artwork uses a gas called neon to make light. It is found on a museum in California. Each side of it is 15 feet long.

Stephen Antonakos, Incomplete Neon Square for La Jolla, *1984, Neon and painted metal, 2 sides, 15' each. Collection of La Jolla Museum of Contemporary Art, Museum Purchase and Modern Art Council Funds.* © *Stephen Antonakos 1984.*

Making Art

1. For this lesson you will make art that's as big as you are. You will need a partner to help you. You will work together to draw **silhouettes**, or outline drawings, of each other.

2. Stand in front of the large sheet of paper on the wall. Turn the light on so your shadow is on the paper. Have your partner tell you how to stand. Your shadow should look interesting. You might want to pretend to do something: shoot a basketball, hold a puppy, run, etc.

3. Now your partner can use a marker to draw the outlines of your shadow. When your silhouette is done, you draw your partner's silhouette on a new sheet of paper.

4. Cut out your silhouette. Then use crayons or markers to add details

to it. Fill in the face and the hair. Add clothes and shoes. If your picture shows you doing something, make sure the details fit the action.

5. Save your life sized **self-portrait**, or drawing of yourself. Your class can hang up all of them for the next parents' night at school. How could you group them to create an interesting, unified artwork?

Art Materials

Large sheets of wrapping paper

Floodlights

Markers

Crayons

41 *Chinese Paper Art*

Looking and Thinking

More than 2,000 years ago the ancient Chinese began making paper. They found they could do many things with paper. If they wet it and mashed it, they could shape it into toys and paper objects. Objects made from paper which has been soaked are called **papier-mâché**.

You are going to make a sculpture of papier-mâché. Your sculpture will be of an imaginary animal. This animal is long and a little like a huge snake, except that it has two sets of legs. It has scales and horns, and it breathes fire. Chinese artists have made many sculptures and paintings of this animal. It is China's national symbol. What is this powerful and all-seeing animal? It is a dragon.

Hsueh Shao-Tang, Dragon, *from* Magic World of Fantasy *by David Duncan, 1978. Reproduced with permission of Harcourt Brace Jovanovich.*

This dragon was made from thousands of stamps torn into little bits. Can you name the parts of the dragon?

This dragon decorates a robe. What other things might the Chinese have decorated with dragons?

China, Early Ching Dynasty, Dragon Robe (detail), 17th century, Silk gauze embroidered with silk. The Metropolitan Museum of Art

Making Art

1. Tear newspaper into strips that look like long bandages.

2. Bend a coat hanger until it looks like the backbone of a dragon. Make it have humps.

3. Crumple two or more paper bags into long narrow shapes. Tape them around the backbone. Tape the bags tighter at the tail. Make a tennis ball of a crumpled bag for the head. Tape it on. Make front legs and back legs from rolled newspapers.

4. Dip the strips of newspaper into starch. Wipe them between your fingers and smooth them over the bags. Cover your dragon from head to tail until you cannot see the bags. Pet him with your wet, starchy hands. Make all the paper stick to him. Let him dry in a warm, safe place.

5. Decide how to show the dragon's eyes and nostrils. You may want to add more newspapers, or you may want to glue on three-dimensional objects. Also give your dragon a square lower jaw.

6. Cover him with more wet newspaper strips. Carefully smooth strips to hold his eyes, nostrils, and jaw to his head. Let him dry.

7. Now tear paper towels into strips. Cover your dragon with his last wet coat. Make him very smooth.

8. When the dragon dries, paint him with bright colors of paint. Do you remember what kinds of colors Oriental artists use? Make your dragon look powerful. Remember he is a national symbol.

Art Materials ◆ THINK SAFETY

Newspapers	Masking tape
Wire coat hanger	Paper towels
Starch	Brush
Paper bags	Paints

42 *Your American Story*

Looking and Thinking

What will you be when you grow up? What will you do? One day you will help your country by the work you do. You don't have to be an astronaut or the president to help America. You can help America by doing any job that needs to be done. Every person who lives in the United States is important to it.

Artist unknown, General Washington on a White Charger, *first half 19th century, Wood, 38⅛" x 29⅜", National Gallery of Art, Washington, Gift of Edgar William and Bernice Chrysler Garbisch.*

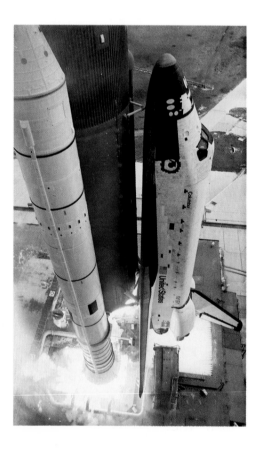

For this lesson you will show yourself as an American. You will draw a self-portrait. Think about the ways you can and will help the country. Decide how to show the kind of work you will do. This will be the background of the artwork. You will draw this part first. The foreground will be your face.

A student artist drew this self-portrait. What work does she want to do? What American symbols does she show?

Making Art

1. Draw an **oval** in the center of a piece of drawing paper. Make your oval as big as your hand.

2. Use crayons to draw in the background for your self-portrait. Remember to make it show the kind of work you will do. Add American symbols to show what country you will be helping. What colors would help you show this?

3. Now fill in the face. The parts of most people's faces are in certain places. Put the eyes in the middle of the oval. Put the nose halfway between the eyes and the chin. Add the mouth under the nose. The ears should go from the eyebrows to the nose.

4. Make the face look like you. Make the eyes and hair the right colors. Draw the hair the way your hair looks. Color the skin to match your skin.

5. Study the picture when it's finished. Could you make it better? Are the background objects the right sizes? Are there details missing from the foreground? Think about freckles, eyelashes, and other parts of your face. Add more background details, too, if you like.

Art Materials

Drawing paper

Crayons

43 *Art To Live In*

Looking and Thinking

An **architect** is a person who designs buildings. There are many steps in designing a building. First the architect has to have ideas. He or she usually has to know things like what the building is for, how many rooms are needed, and where the building will be. These facts help the architect decide what kinds of things the building must have. Once the architect has ideas, he or she draws several sketches of the building. Changes are made until the drawing meets all the requirements. Then a fine copy, called a **blueprint**, is made of the drawing. From the blueprint the architect often builds a model. The model is tested and shown to people. Only then does the real building get built.

Braldt Bralds, Untitled. Commissioned by the Design School/Art Institute of Dallas.

Remember that three-dimensional forms make buildings. Can you name the forms in this picture? Can you see them in the buildings in the background?

These pictures are of a very famous old building and a very famous new building. Which is which?

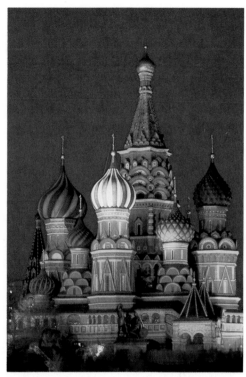

Making Art

1. Think of a design for a special building in which children could play. What things should the building have? Will it need many rooms or one big room? Will it need lots of windows or doors? How will it look from the outside? Where will it be? What forms can the building have that will make it look interesting? Plan your building carefully. Use a pencil to sketch your ideas.

2. Now make your final drawing. Make it look like a blueprint. Use white construction paper and blue chalk. Draw the lines and forms of your building. Make the different parts of the building the right sizes.

3. Add the details of the building. Think of all the things you have seen on the outsides of buildings. Which of these things does your building need?

4. When your blueprint is done, share it with a classmate. Tell where your building will be. Point out all the special parts of your building. See if your classmate can think of anything to add.

Art Materials

Pencil

Drawing paper

White construction paper

Blue chalk

95

44 Art That Shows Ideas and Feelings

Looking and Thinking

Study the two paintings in this lesson. How are they alike? How are they different? How do you feel when you look at the painting below? How do you feel when you look at the other painting?

Helen Frankenthaler, Small's Paradise, 1964, Acrylic on canvas, 100" x 93⅝". National Museum of American Art (formerly National Collection of Fine Arts), Smithsonian Institution, Gift of George L. Erion. 1967.121

Art like the two paintings in this lesson is called **nonobjective** art. Nonobjective paintings do not tell a story or try to look real. Instead, paint and color are used to get across a feeling or idea. What ideas and feelings do the two paintings in this lesson show?

Lee Krasner, Between Two Appearances, *1981, Oil on canvas with paper collage, 47" × 57¼". Robert Miller Gallery, Inc., New York.*

Making Art

1. How do you feel today? What colors would show how you feel? Choose three colors of paint.

2. Spread newspapers on the floor. You need to work on the floor because you will use large paper. Also choose a large brush to use with your paints.

3. Make a nonobjective painting. Paint the way you feel. Use smooth strokes or jagged strokes. Fill in large spaces with single colors, or mix up the colors. You can even let your paint drip off your brush as you shake it over the paper. Also leave blank spaces if that is how you feel. Just be sure to use your paints and brush to show your feelings.

4. When your painting is finished, let it dry. Use words to write how you feel today. Share both your words and your painting with a friend. Which tells your feelings better?

Art Materials
Butcher paper
Paints
Large brush

97

45 *Art That Moves*

Looking and Thinking

Do you like to watch television? What's your favorite show? What do you like best about the show?

A television show starts out as a story. Television producers, or people who make the shows, look for certain things in stories. They have studied what people who watch television like to see. Think about the kinds of stories your favorite shows have.

Once a producer likes a story, people must be chosen to play the parts. Television producers usually look for certain types of people for the parts. Do your favorite television characters fit their parts?

Many more important decisions are made before a television show is filmed. Filming is the last step. The picture below shows a television show being filmed. Would you like to be there?

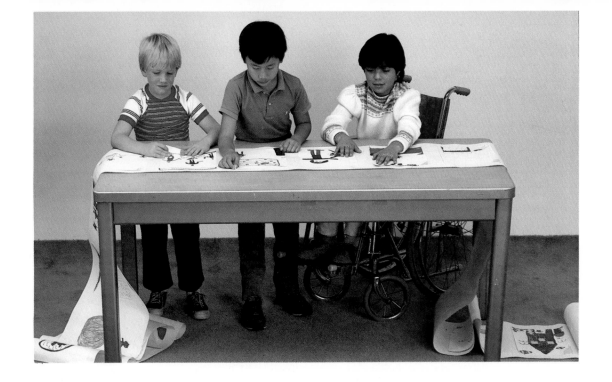

Making Art

1. Your class can make a television show. You can all be producers. First, listen carefully to the story your teacher reads aloud. Decide together how to show the story on television. Instead of filming real characters, you will draw a **storyboard**. A storyboard shows what will happen in a film. Each of you will draw a picture to show a part of the story. You need to choose as many parts in the story as there are students in the class.

2. Choose the special part that you will draw. Use felt markers to show what's happening in your part of the story. Remember to use lines, shapes, and colors that fit the mood of the story.

3. When all the pictures are done, work together to put them in order. They should go from what happens first to what happens last.

Glue them in order from left to right on the long sheet of butcher paper. Leave a space on the left end and a space on the right end. Work together to draw a title for the left end. Write all your names at the right end of the film. You are all the producers.

4. Now you can wind the film around the rollers inside the television box. Your teacher will help you. Someone can crank the film through as the story is read aloud. Different people should read the different parts. Will your television show be a winner?

Art Materials		THINK SAFETY
Drawing paper	Butcher paper	
Felt markers		
Glue	Box	
	Rollers	

Exploring Art

African Art

In this unit you have learned about many cultures' special art styles. You have learned why different cultures make different kinds of art. One important type of art you have not learned much about is African art.

There are many kinds of African art. One interesting kind is made from wood. (Why do you suppose wood is used?) From wood African artists carve household items. They make objects like spoons, bowls, and vases. They make the objects look interesting or richly decorated. The objects below are examples.

You can be an African artist. Think of a household object that has a boring design. How could you make this object into a work of art? Think of a design that could be carved out of wood. Then draw your design on a sheet of paper. Draw more designs as you have more ideas. Put them together to make an African art design **portfolio**. A portfolio is a collection of an artist's work.

Review

Knowing About Art

Helen Frankenthaler, Small's Paradise, *1964, Acrylic on canvas, 100" x 93⅝." National Museum of American Art (formerly National Collection of Fine Arts), Smithsonian Institution, Gift of George L. Erion. 1967. 121*

Courtesy Department Library Services, American Museum of Natural History. Neg. No. 273397

1. Which piece of art was made first? How can you tell?

2. What was used to make each piece of art?

3. Which piece of art is about ideas and feelings? Which piece of art tells a story?

4. Tell about the style of each piece of art.

5. What do you like best about each piece of art?

Unit 4

Art for Every Day

Every day, all around the world, children like you create art. They make all different kinds of art. They use all kinds of art materials. Can you think of some kinds of art children in other lands might create? Do you think most children would enjoy creating a mural like the one below?

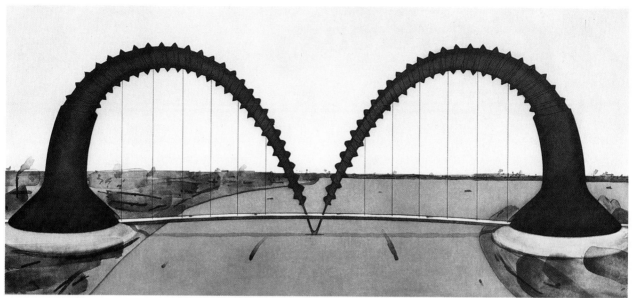

Claes Oldenburg, Screwarch Bridge, 1980, Etching and aquatint, 23¹¹/₁₆" x 50¾." Collection, The Museum of Modern Art, New York, Gift of Klaus G. Perls and Heinz Berggruen in memory of Frank Perls, Art Dealer.

Famous artists also make all kinds of art. They use many kinds of art materials. But the most important thing they use is imagination. The artist of this picture used his imagination. How does it show?

When you use your imagination, you can see art everywhere. You can think of unusual ways to use common objects. You can also improve everyday objects so they become true pieces of art. How could you use the things in this picture to create art? Is the picture itself art? Think about what you see. How can you add art to your daily life? This unit will give you some ideas.

46 *Art from Scraps*

Looking and Thinking

Think of all the things you have used this year to make art. Were you surprised that some of these things worked? Art can be made from almost anything. A single piece of art can also have many different materials in it. Study the artwork below. It is a collage that shows a real-life scene. How many different materials do you see in it?

Romare Bearden, Blue Interior, Morning, 1968, Collage on board, 44" x 56". From the Collection of the Chase Manhattan Bank, N.A.

This collage is made of many materials. But it still has a center of interest. What is it?

How many different materials do you see in this collage? The name of this artwork is *Cherry Picture.* Can you see why? What is the center of interest?

Kurt Schwitters, Cherry Picture, 1921, Collage of colored papers, fabrics, printed labels and pictures, pieces of wood, etc., and gouache on cardboard background, 36⅛" x 27¾". Collection, The Museum of Modern Art, New York, Mr. and Mrs. Atwater Kent, Jr. Fund.

Making Art

1. Think of a real-life scene you could show in a collage. Make sure your idea has a center of interest. This will help all the small, different pieces of the collage work together as a whole.

2. Collect man-made scraps and objects from nature. Decide for which parts of your picture each kind of material will work best. You might want to use paints and crayons as well. Arrange all of your objects on a sheet of paper so that they show your idea. Remember to have a center of interest. Glue down all the objects and scraps. Use paints or crayons where you planned to.

3. Give your collage a title. Choose a name that tells about your center of interest. See if a friend can find all the different materials in your picture.

Art Materials THINK SAFETY

Paper

Objects from nature

Man-made scraps

Glue

Paints or crayons

47 Garden in a Box

Looking and Thinking

Do you have a garden at home? There are many kinds of gardens. There are green gardens like the one below. There are gardens where vegetables and fruits are grown. There are flower gardens like the one on the next page. There are even tiny gardens inside jars and window boxes. What kind of garden would you like to have?

Today you will make your own garden in a box. You will be creating a type of artwork called a **diorama**. A diorama is a miniature, or very small, realistic scene. Usually a diorama includes a background that looks real and small sculptures that fit the setting. You will create the setting today. In the next lesson you will create the sculptures.

Making Art

1. Think about the colors your garden will have. Will it be all different shades of green? Will it have many bright colors to show flowers? Will it have the colors of fruits and vegetables? Decide on five or six colors. Then choose tissue paper in these colors.

2. Tear each sheet of tissue paper into many small pieces. Keep your colors in separate piles.

3. Divide the inside of your box into eight sections. You will work on one section at a time. Dip your brush into the starch, and paint the first section.

4. Cover the starch with tissue paper. Overlap the pieces. Put the light colors behind the dark colors.

5. Do all eight sections of the box. Use your fingers to smooth down all the pieces.

6. Let your box dry. Then see how it looks. What happened where two colors overlapped? How many colors does your garden have?

Art Materials

Shoe box

Starch

Brush

Tissue paper

48 *What Belongs in a Garden?*

Looking and Thinking

Today you will add to your diorama. You will use clay to make small figures, animals, or other things you might see in a garden. You will create **additive sculpture**.

Additive sculpture is made when pieces are joined together. Clay is especially easy to use for additive sculpture. You can join pieces of clay by pressing them together and then smoothing the joint. Study the pictures below to see how.

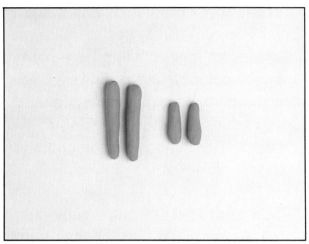

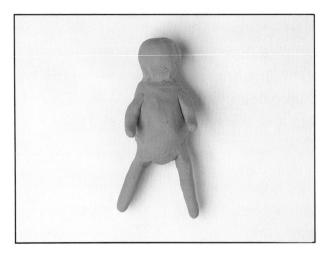

These figures are made of metal, not clay. Can you see how the pieces were joined together? Look at the figure on the left. Notice how the arms, legs, and feet all look like they were added to the main body. Look at the figure on the right. The main piece is the head, body, and right leg. What small pieces were added?

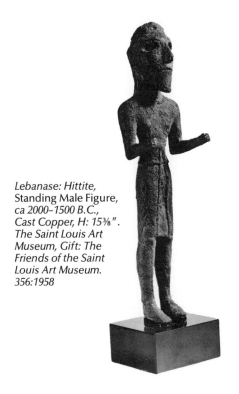

Lebanase: Hittite, Standing Male Figure, ca 2000–1500 B.C., Cast Copper, H: 15⅜". The Saint Louis Art Museum, Gift: The Friends of the Saint Louis Art Museum. 356:1958

Alexander Archipenko, The Gondolier. The Metropolitan Museum of Art, New York, Gift of Ernst Anspach, 1964.

Making Art

1. Think of two sculptures you'd like to add to your garden. They could show people, animals, or things like benches and tree trunks. Use your imagination to think of things that could go in a garden. Decide what sizes your sculptures should be to best fit in the space of your garden.

2. Use clay to make your sculptures. Form the large pieces first. Then make the small pieces.

3. Join the pieces together. Use your fingers to smooth the joint where two pieces meet.

4. Place your sculptures in the garden. What else could you add to your garden to make it better?

Art Materials
Clay

49 Pictures Help Poems

Looking and Thinking

The poem below was written by Eve Merriam. Read the poem, and look at the pictures in this lesson. Do they go together?

> Landscape
>
> What will you find at the edge of the world?
> A footprint,
> a feather,
> desert sand swirled?
> A tree of ice,
> a rain of stars,
> or a junkyard of cars?
>
> What will there be at the rim of the earth?
> A mollusc,
> a mammal,
> a new creature's birth?
> Eternal sunrise,
> immortal sleep,
> or cars piled up in a rusty heap?
>
> *Eve Merriam*

Pictures that go with stories or poems are called **illustrations**. The pictures in this lesson are photographs, not illustrations. How would you illustrate Eve Merriam's poem?

Making Art

1. What do you think is at the edge of the world? It doesn't have to be something talked about in the poem. Use your imagination to decide what you think is there. Write down your idea.

2. Make a picture that shows your idea. Use paper and whatever art materials will work best for your idea.

3. Show your picture to a friend. Tell about what is found at the edge of the world.

Art Materials
Paper
Crayons, paints, markers, pencil, etc.

50 *What Does a Desert Look Like?*

Looking and Thinking

Have you ever been to a desert? About 1/7 of the earth is covered with deserts. The Sahara is the world's largest desert. It is in northern Africa. This desert is 3 1/2 million square miles. That's almost as big as our whole country!

The pictures on these two pages should help you see what a desert is like. A desert is very hot, dry, and sandy. Deserts are not always flat, though. The center of the Sahara has mountains nearly 10,000 feet high. The Sahara also has rocky plateaus (hills with flat tops) and plains made of gravel. Miles and miles of flat areas filled with sand are called *ergs.* The wind sweeps the sand from the ergs into big mounds called *dunes.* The Sahara also has about 90 places where grass and trees grow. These areas are called *oases.* They are spots of green in the huge, sand-colored desert.

Can you see how the wind has moved the sand in the photograph above? Why are there so few plants?

How does the sky contrast with the desert in these photographs?

Making Art

1. As a class you are going to make a **mural** showing the desert. A mural is a very big picture. Today you will paint only the background. Talk about how it should look. You will want to show the sky. You will also want to show the different parts of a desert. What are these?

2. Work together to sketch the outlines of your desert. Plan the spaces of the mural carefully. Show where the sky will meet the land. This is the horizon. Show mountains, plateaus, and ergs. What else will you show?

3. Choose the colors you will use to paint the background. Each of you can work on a small area of the big mural. Which part do you want to paint? Work as a group to make the small parts of the mural blend together.

Art Materials
Mural paper
Pencil
Paints
Brush

113

51 *What Belongs in a Desert?*

Looking and Thinking

Part of the Sahara lies in the country called Egypt. The desert of Egypt has some famous things in it. The picture below shows the Sphinx and a Pyramid. These huge stone structures were built 4,500 years ago. They are amazing works of art. They are huge, yet were built by men using only the simplest of tools.

A famous river called the Nile is also found winding through the Sahara in Egypt. Along the Nile are oases like this one. What is in the oasis? A desert has very few plants outside of oases. Right after rain falls, however, bright and beautiful flowers grow all over the desert.

People who live in the Sahara usually wander from place to place looking for water. They live in tents and wear long robes. These people often own sheep, goats, and camels. Wild animals such as snakes, mice, lizards, rabbits, and wolves also live in the desert.

Making Art

1. Think of all the things that are found in the Sahara. Choose one of which you would like to make a picture. You can add your picture to the class mural. It will be part of the foreground.

2. Look at the background of the mural. Decide how big your foreground piece should be. Then draw the outlines of it. Use pencil and white construction paper.

3. Use crayons to color your drawing.

4. Use scissors to cut out your picture.

5. Work as a class to decide where each picture should go on the mural. Then use glue to put your picture where it belongs.

6. As a class, decide where to hang your mural. You want many people to enjoy it. A bank, store, or office building might be a good place.

Art Materials	THINK SAFETY
White construction paper	Scissors
Pencil	Glue
Crayons	

52 Lines That Move

Looking and Thinking

Do you read comic books or newspaper comic strips? Who is your favorite character? Ten years ago many children your age liked Batman and Robin. They are shown below. Have you ever seen these characters?

Can you tell what Batman and Robin are doing? It looks like they are moving, doesn't it? Comic book artists are good at showing action.

When you watch television cartoons, you really do see movement. Cartoon artists call the art of showing movement **animation**. They create animation by drawing many, many pictures of the same thing. Each picture is a little bit different. All the pictures are quickly shown one after the other. The small changes look like movement.

How does this cartoon show movement?

©1985 Bhob Productions/Kevin Dixey.

Making Art

1. You can make cards that show movement. Put them together to make a flip book.

2. Decide what you will show moving. Choose a simple idea. A person waving his or her hand is one idea. You can show movement just by changing where the hand is on the pictures.

3. Lay five index cards side-by-side on your desk. Make the drawings for the first and last cards. These will show the beginning and end of the action. Draw with a black marker, and use simple lines.

4. Now make the drawings for the rest of the cards. The middle card should show what happens right in the middle of the action. The second and fourth cards should show small changes.

5. Stack your cards in order. The first card should go on the bottom. The last card should go on the top.

6. Hold the stack of cards tightly in one hand. Use the thumb of your other hand to flip through the cards. Flip from bottom to top. Can you see the movement?

Art Materials
Index cards
Black marker

117

53 *The Art of Advertising*

Looking and Thinking

The world is full of advertisements. Advertisements try to sell us things. Think of all the advertisements you see during a television show. Think of billboards along the highway. Think of movie posters. There are also advertisements in magazines and newspapers. Even radios have advertisements that you can hear.

Graphic designers create art for advertisements. Below is a poster with simple graphic art. What do you like best about a simple design like this?

Courtesy of Peter Good Graphic Design, Chester, Connecticut.

This is a **trademark** for a water park. A trademark is a company's own symbol. A company uses a trademark a little like a nickname. People see the trademark and think of the company. Trademarks are like small advertisements. Can you tell what Wild Waters is like by looking at the trademark?

Courtesy of Leisure Attractions Advertising, Inc., Silver Springs, Florida.

Making Art

1. Think of a place you like to visit. It could be an imaginary place, too. What's fun about this place? Think how you could show it in a simple graphic. You should create a design that will make others want to visit the place.

2. Sketch your idea for a simple design. If you create a trademark, try to make all the letters look like they belong together.

3. Color your design with crayons. Choose bright colors that people will notice best.

4. See if the class has ideas that would make your design better.

Art Materials
Paper
Pencil
Crayons

54 *Frame It!*

Looking and Thinking

You have made prints this year with your thumb and with a piece of clay. The high parts made the print when covered with paint. The low parts did not print. There is a type of printing you can do without worrying about the low and high parts of the printing object. This kind of printing is done with a **stencil**.

A stencil is a sheet of stiff paper with a shape cut out of it. Below are some stencils made by student artists like you.

Making Art

1. Choose a picture you made this year. You are going to decorate a frame for it. First **mount** the picture on a stiff piece of paper bigger than the picture is. Your teacher will help you place the picture in the middle. Glue it down smoothly. Notice how the big piece of paper forms a frame.

2. Now use scissors and a small piece of stiff paper to create a stencil. Make sure the shape you cut out of the paper is small enough to fit on the frame.

3. Choose a color of crayon that looks good with your picture. Gently use the crayon to color in the stencil. Place your stencil all around the frame as you work. Try to make the stencil prints have equal spaces between them. This will create rhythm.

4. Does the frame make your artwork look more complete? Choose other artworks that you'd like to frame. Try different colors and designs for your stencil prints.

Art Materials	THINK SAFETY
Your own artwork	Crayons
Stiff paper (large pieces and small squares)	Scissors
	Glue

55 Patterns for Fabrics

Looking and Thinking

One way to make designs in fabrics is to **weave** together different colors and types of thread. But some pieces of fabric are woven from only one color and type of thread. How do these pieces get designs on them?

Block printing works well to put designs on cloth. A block holds together the raised parts of a design. The block can be used over and over to make a pattern of prints. The piece of cloth below has a repeated print on it. What would the block look like? Remember that only the raised parts of a block make the print.

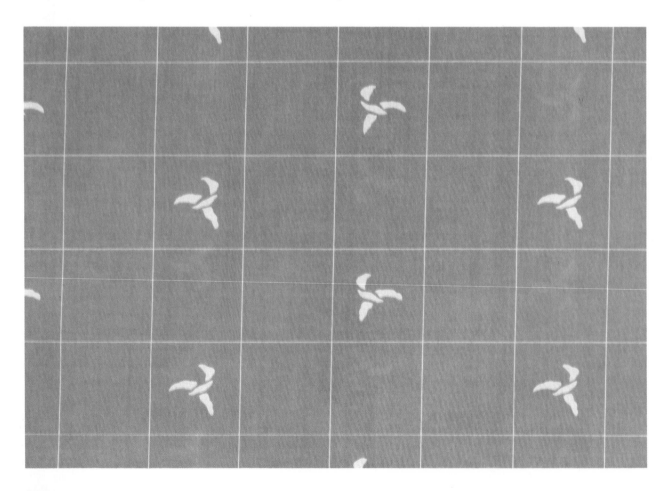

Making Art

1. Create a design that would work well as a block print. The design can be one piece, or it can be several smaller shapes.

2. Cut up a styrofoam cup to make your design.

3. Glue your styrofoam pieces to a thick piece of cardboard.

4. Press your printing block against a sponge filled with paint. Bright colors of paint will work best. Press the block against a piece of cloth. Does the print look like you thought it would?

5. Keep making prints on your piece of fabric. Arrange them in a pattern that you like. You could make the prints in rows to show rhythm. Or you could scatter the prints across the piece of fabric. Try to make every print clear. Use several colors if you want to.

Art Materials

Styrofoam cup	Paint
Thick piece of cardboard	Scissors
Cloth	Sponge

56 Spatter It!

Looking and Thinking

Jackson Pollock was an important American painter. Since he painted in a new way, he was called an **original** painter. His style of painting was liked by many other artists. Together they created an art style called **Abstract Expressionism**.

The painting below is one of Pollock's most famous. It is an example of Abstract Expressionism. He did the painting in 1950. Pollock painted by dripping, pouring, spattering, and even throwing paint on a canvas. How do you think he applied the black paint as he made this painting?

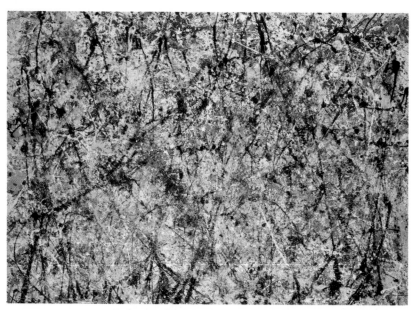

Jackson Pollock, Number 1, 1950 (Lavender Mist), 1950, Oil, enamel, and aluminum on canvas, 87" x 118". National Gallery of Art, Washington, Ailsa Mellon Bruce Fund.

This painting is very large. It measures over 7 feet high by 9 feet long. Pollock laid it on the floor and walked around it as he painted it. Why wouldn't it work to prop the canvas up to paint it?

You will do spatter painting today. You won't use as big a canvas as Jackson Pollock did. What do you like about this spatter painting by a student artist?

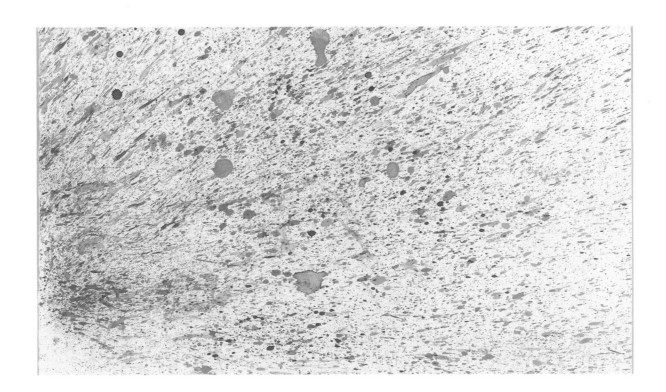

Making Art

1. Choose three colors of paint that look good together.

2. Slide a sheet of white paper under the wire screen.

3. Dip a toothbrush into the paint. Get lots of paint on the toothbrush.

4. Rake the toothbrush across the wire screen. Spatter all three colors in this way. Do you like the way the colors look together? What do you think about creating art in this way?

5. Now use the paint and the toothbrush to create a realistic drawing. Use the toothbrush like a paintbrush to make quick strokes of color. Compare your two artworks. Tell how they are alike and different. Tell which way of working pleased you most as an artist.

Art Materials	THINK SAFETY
Paint	
Toothbrush	
Wire screen	
Paper	

57 *Weaving, Looms, and Table Mats*

Looking and Thinking

You have learned that cloth is made when pieces of thread are woven over and under other pieces of thread. Most weaving today is done on huge machines called **looms**. These machines can make a great deal of cloth very quickly. However, a few people still weave by hand on small looms. The cloth made this way is very special. It is usually made by the hands of just one person.

National Symbol of Mexico, *Weaving, 1880s. Courtesy of San Diego Museum of Man.*

Today you will make and use your own loom. You will make a special piece of cloth by hand.

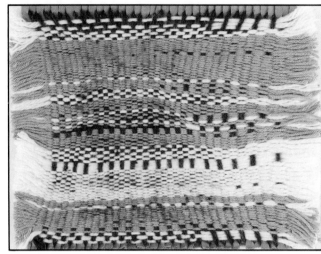

Making Art

1. Mark the two short ends of a piece of cardboard every 1/4 inch. Your teacher will show you how to use the ruler.

2. Use your scissors to make a small cut where each mark is.

3. Wind string tightly around the cardboard. Take it through each notch to the one across from it. Work from one side of the loom to the other. Pull the string tight. Cut the string and stick it down in back with tape.

4. Now take colorful pieces of yarn and work them over and under the string. Push each piece of yarn tightly up against those above it. Remember that if a piece of yarn begins *over*, the next piece should begin *under*.

5. Think about the colors of yarn as you weave them. Plan which look good side-by-side. If you want to, make a regular pattern in your weaving. You could use two strands of one color, one strand of another, then two strands of the first. This will create a pattern that has rhythm. Decide what will work best for your weaving. Fill the whole piece of cardboard with it.

Art Materials

THINK SAFETY

Cardboard	Scissors
Pencil	String
Ruler	Colored yarn
Tape	

58 Clowns Make You Laugh

Looking and Thinking

Have you ever seen a clown? Clowns are funny to watch. They use art to make themselves look funny. They dress in strange clothes and mix up colors and patterns. They paint funny faces on themselves. Clowns also do funny things. Maybe you've even dressed up like a clown or acted like one. If so, you probably had fun making others laugh.

What makes these clowns funny?

Student artists made these clowns. What makes them funny? Study the colors, shapes, and textures used.

Making Art

1. You can use what you know about art to create a funny clown. A popsicle stick can hold all the parts of your clown together. Fold strips of paper like you folded the fan in Lesson 14. These make bouncy arms and legs that move in funny ways. Use your imagination to do the the rest!

2. Think about colors. What warm colors would make people feel happy? What colors would look strange next to one another? Think about the colors a clown should have.

3. Think about lines. What lines can you use to show a light, happy mood? Where on the clown will you use them?

4. Think about shapes. How many different shapes can you use to create your clown?

5. Think about texture. How can you give your clown texture? Can you put textures side-by-side to create a funny effect?

6. Make a list of the art materials you will need. Have your teacher help you gather them together. Then make that clown!

Art Materials

Popsicle stick

1" paper strips

Your choice

59 *What Kind of Artist Are You?*

Looking and Thinking

Cats have been favorite subjects of artists and writers throughout time. Cats can do special things that other animals cannot. They see very well in the dark. They can climb, run, and jump farther and more quickly than many animals. They can easily walk along narrow ledges. If they should fall, they usually land on their feet. Cats are also very skilled hunters. People throughout history have admired cats for these talents. The ancient Egyptians even worshiped cats.

Cats are also mysterious. They are very independent. Some people fear cats because they do not understand them. Do you think the cats below are scary? Why do you say so?

An artist named Paul Klee often drew cats like this one. What is the cat thinking? What would it like to do?

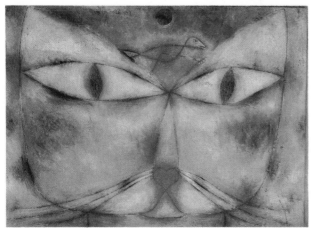

Paul Klee, Cat and Bird, *1928, Oil and ink on gesso on canvas, mounted on wood, 15" × 21". Collection, The Museum of Modern Art, New York, The Sidney and Harriet Janis Collection Fund, and gift of Suzy Prudden Sussman and Joan H. Meijer in memory of F. H. Hirschland.*

These cats were made by student artists like you. What do you like best about each cat?

Making Art

1. You are an artist. You can create any kind of cat you want to. You can create a soft, sculptured cat by stuffing a sock to give it form. You can carve a cat. You can make a cat wire sculpture. You can draw or paint a cat. You can create a printing block that shows a cat. Think of all the art projects you know how to do. Use your artistic imagination to choose one way to make an artwork that has a cat as the center of interest.

2. Plan your artwork first. Then use the medium you have chosen to create your artwork. Use your art materials correctly. Follow your plan.

3. Share your completed artwork with the class. Tell why you chose the medium you used. Tell what you liked best about working on your cat. Tell what was hardest to do. Sign your artwork. You are the artist.

Art Materials THINK SAFETY

Your choice

60 *Putting on an Art Show*

Looking and Thinking

Where can you go to see famous works of art? **Art museums** are places that care for and show artworks. Most big cities have museums. Two famous ones are the Louvre in Paris, France, and the Metropolitan Museum of Art in New York City. Even small cities have small museums called **galleries**. Here you can see and often buy artworks.

Museums themselves are works of art. They are often beautiful to see. The pictures below show the Metropolitan Museum of Art (right) and the Guggenheim Museum (left). They are both in New York City. Which do you think was built last? Why?

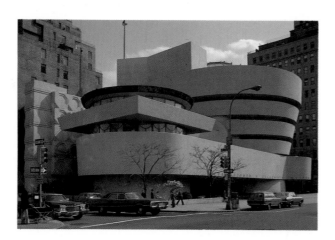

The insides of museums are important, too. The picture on the right is of an **exhibit**, or special art show, in Italy. The picture on the left was taken at the Museum of Fine Arts in Boston. Do you like the way the artworks are shown?

Making Art

1. Your class can put on its own show. First you must choose your favorite artwork from this year.

2. Decide if your artwork needs any finishing touches. You might want to **mount** and **frame** it. Lesson 54 can help you to do this.

3. Work as a class to decide how to group the artworks. You might want to put all the paintings together; all the sculptures together, and all the prints together. Or you might group the artworks by color or one of the other elements of art. Decide how the artworks will look best.

4. Hang white sheets along one wall of your classroom. Pin your artworks to the sheets. Under each artwork, print the title of it and the name of the artist. Use index cards. If there are sculptures, set them on tables covered with white sheets.

5. Decide if the lighting is good enough. If you need to, shine lights right on your exhibit.

6. Invite people to come and see your art show.

Art Materials	

Your own artwork

Mounting and framing materials

White sheets

Pins

Index cards

Pens

Lights

133

Exploring Art

A Summer Diary

What will you do this summer? Will you play or read or help around the house? Will you go on a trip or stay at home? What are your plans?

Someday you might want to remember all the fun things you do this summer. A diary will help you to remember. A diary is a book that you write. It tells what you do every day.

You will better remember what you do if you have pictures. You can illustrate your diary. Then you can tell *and* show what you do.

You can use a notebook for your diary. You can also make your own diary. Your teacher will show you how. Get ready to be the author and illustrator of your own book!

Review

Valuing Art

Pablo Picasso, Three Musicians, 1921 (summer), Oil on canvas, 6'7" x 7' 3¾."
Collection, The Museum of Modern Art, New York, Mrs. Simon Guggenheim
Fund.

1. Name the elements of art. Can you find examples of each in this painting?

2. What do you see in the painting? Can you find the dog?

3. Do you like this style of painting? Why or why not?

4. What do you like best about the painting? What do you like least?

5. Pablo Picasso painted this picture. He is thought to be one of the greatest modern artists. Find out more about him. Write a short report about Picasso.

Glossary

Abstract Expressionism /ab′-strakt′ ik-spresh′-ə-niz′-əm/ A modern style of painting. The artist shows feelings and ideas by dripping, pouring, spattering, or throwing paint on a canvas.

additive sculpture Made by joining together materials.

advertisement /ad′-vər-tiz′mənt/ A printed or spoken message meant to make people want to buy or do something.

animation Moving art made by putting many pictures together. Each picture shows a small change in movement. When the pictures are all shown quickly one after the other, the objects in the pictures seem to move.

architect /är′-kə′tekt/ An artist who designs buildings.

art gallery A place where people can see and sometimes buy artworks.

art museum A building where artworks are shown and cared for.

background Parts of a picture that look farther away or behind other objects.

balance When all sides of an artwork go together to create a sense of evenness.

bark painting A type of art created by the Aborigines over 40,000 years ago. Paints were made from plants. Then designs were painted on bark.

blend To mix colors together. Also to move smoothly from one color to another without making a line.

block printing Printing a design on paper or fabric. A block with a raised design on its surface is used to make the print.

blueprint A fine copy of an architect's plan for a building.

cave painting Pictures painted on cave walls almost 40,000 years ago. They often show animals and tell stories.

center of interest The most important part in a work of art.

coil A long, skinny shape like a rope made from clay. Clay coils can be used to make pottery.

collage /kə-läzh′/ An artwork made from a variety of objects. They are joined together by gluing them to a flat surface.

color The quality that makes something red, green, orange, yellow, or so on.

color wheel A circle divided into sections of different colors. It shows how colors can be mixed or used together.

cool colors Blue, green, violet, and their related colors.

decorate To add lines, colors, shapes, and textures to objects. Decoration can make objects more detailed or pleasing to the eye.

detail A small part of a whole.

diorama /di′-ə-ram′-ə/ A miniature artwork that includes a realistic background and three-dimensional foreground objects. Seeing a diorama is like looking at a tiny, real scene.

elements of art The important things artists see in the world. These are put together to create an artwork. Line, shape, space, texture, color, and value are elements of design.

exhibit /ig-zib′-ət/ A special show of a group of artworks.

fabric Cloth; made by weaving threads together.

foreground The part of a picture that looks closest. It is usually noticed first.

form Created when shapes are joined together to enclose space. A form can be measured from top to bottom, side to side, and front to back.

frame To mount a picture and put a stiff rim of cardboard, wood, or other material around it.

graphic designer A person who creates art for advertisements, packages, signs, books, magazines, and so on.

horizon The line where water or land seems to end and the sky begins.

illustrations /il′-əs-trā′-shən/ Pictures that help tell a story or explain what is said.

Impressionism /im-presh′-ə-niz-əm/ Art that tries to show the way light changes objects and colors. Impressionist artists use dots of color placed closely together.

landscape A picture of an outdoor scene.

line A path that a point has followed.

loom A frame used for weaving cloth. Some threads are held by the loom while other threads are woven through them.

media The materials used by an artist.

model A small artwork that shows how a larger object, such as a plane or house, might look.

mold A hollow form that is filled with soft material. When the material hardens, the mold is removed. The material is a copy of the mold.

monochromatic /män′-ə-krō-mat′-ik/ Using one color, including its tints and its shades.

mood The feeling created by a work of art.

mosaic /mō-zā′-ik/ A picture made by fitting together tiny pieces of colored tiles, stones, paper, or other materials.

mount To attach a picture to a larger piece of paper or cardboard.

mural A large artwork, usually found on a wall.

nearika /nā-är-ē′-kȧ/ Native Mexican art made by filling a surface with colorful yarn.

nonobjective art A modern style of art that does not try to show things as they really look. Instead, artists try to show ideas and feelings.

Oriental art /ōr-ē-ent′-əl/ Art created in Japan, China, and other countries near them. Oriental art often shows flowers, dragons, and butterflies, and uses primary colors.

original Art that is done in a new and different way.

oval Egg-shaped.

overlapping Occurs when parts of an artwork somewhat cover other parts.

papier-mâché /pā-per-mə-shā′/ Strips of paper dipped into paste, starch, or glue. The paper can be molded into shapes and is strong and solid when it dries.

pattern Shapes, lines, or colors used over and over to form a design.

perspective /pər-spek′-tiv/ Showing distance in a picture that is made on a flat surface. Overlapping and size differences help give perspective.

photograph A picture made using a camera and film.

portfolio A collection of an artist's works.

pottery Pots, dishes, vases, and other objects molded from wet clay.

primary colors Red, yellow, and blue. All colors except white are made by mixing these colors.

principles of design Laws or rules that help in making good designs. Balance, contrast, variety, pattern, rhythm, emphasis, and unity are principles of design.

print Made when an object is covered with paint or ink and then pressed against paper. Prints show the raised parts of the surface of the printing object.

puppet A small doll or figure that can be moved.

quilling Art made by covering an object or piece of clothing with porcupine quills colored with dye.

rhythm /rith'-əm/ A regular repeating of lines, shapes, colors, or patterns.

rubbing A design made by rubbing a crayon or soft pencil over a paper covering a textured object.

sculpture A carving or model. Sculptures are three-dimensional.

secondary colors Green, orange, and violet. These colors are made by mixing two *primary colors.*

self-portrait A picture an artist makes of himself or herself.

shade Created when a color is mixed with black or another dark color.

shape A flat figure created when lines meet and enclose space.

silhouette /sil-ə-wet'/ An outline of a shape without any details inside, like a shadow.

space The open parts between or inside shapes and forms.

spiral A curving line that winds around and around toward a center point.

stencil A heavy paper with a design cut out of it. Stencils are used to make prints.

storyboard A board which shows what will happen in each frame of a film.

symbol Something that stands for something else.

symmetry /sim'-ə-trē/ A kind of balance in which the two sides of a picture are exactly alike.

texture The way a surface feels to the touch—smooth, bumpy, rough, slippery, and so on.

three-dimensional /thre'-də-men'-chən-əl/ Having a front and back, top and bottom, and sides. Three-dimensional art has height, width, and depth.

tie-dye Colorful cloth with designs of lines and circles. The designs are made because objects are tied into the cloth with string. The wrapped areas resist the colored dye into which the cloth is dipped.

tint Created when a color is mixed with white.

title A name given to a picture, sculpture, or other artwork.

trademark A symbol used by a company to show something about the company or the things they sell.

unity When all the parts of an artwork look like they belong together.

value The lightness or darkness of a color.

variety /və-rī'-ət-ē/ When things are changed slightly to add interest to an artwork.

warm colors Red, orange, yellow, and their related colors.

warp Threads that go up and down in weaving.

weft In weaving, threads that are woven back and forth through the warp threads.

winter count A record made on animal skin by Indians long ago. It showed pictures of important things that had happened during each year.

woven Made by lacing together pieces of yarn, thread, or other materials.

Artists' Reference

All the artists and artwork presented in this book are listed here. Use this list to locate particular paintings and to find works by artists who especially interest you.

Albers, Anni — *Preliminary Design for Wall Hanging* 46

Antonakos, Stephen — *Incomplete Neon Square for La Jolla* 89

Archipenko, Alexander — *The Gondolier* 109

Azarian, Mary — *December* 81

Bartolommeo, Fra — *Hermitage on a Slope* 39

Bearden, Romare — *Blue Interior, Morning, 1968* 104

Bingham, George Caleb — *Fur Traders Descending the Missouri* 24

Blakelock, Ralph Albert — *Moonlight* 57

Bralds, Braldt — *Untitled* 94

Davis, Stuart — *New York Elevated* 5, 33

Degas — *Little Fourteen-Year-Old Dancer* 65

Delaunay, Robert — *Simultaneous Contrasts: Sun and Moon* 37

El Greco — *View of Toledo* 27

Fragonard, Jean-Honoré — *The Visit to the Nursery* 45, 67

Frankenthaler, Helen — *Small's Paradise* 96, 101

Hasui, Kawase — *Hinomisaki in Moonlight in Izumo Province* 56

Hopper, Edward — *The Long Leg* 43

Horiuchi, Paul — *Mosaic Mural at the Seattle Center* 72

Johnson, Eastman — *The Brown Family* 35

Kandinsky, Vasily — *Open Green* 14
Painting No. 201 21

Klee, Paul — *Cat and Bird* 131

Krasner, Lee — *Between Two Appearances* 97

Lassaw, Ibram — *Corax* 50

Lindstrand, Doug — from *Alaskan Sketchbook* 71

Mondrian, Piet — *Composition, V.* 14

Monet, Claude — *Cliffs of Pourville, Morning* 38

Moore, Henry — *Figures in a Setting* 44

Naha, Helen — *Hopi Wedding Vase*   79
Nampeyo, Rachel — *Hopi Jar*   78
Oldenburg, Claes — *Geometric Mouse Scale A*   88
Screwarch Bridge   103

Ouchi, Michi — *Hanabi (Fireworks)*   84
Parrott, Alice — *La Mesa*   12
Picasso, Pablo — *Three Musicians*   135
Pollock, Jackson — *Number 1, 1950 (Lavender Mist)*   124
Prutscher, Otto — *Wine Goblet*   68
Redon, Odilon — *Vase of Flowers*   23
Ruscha, Ed — *Annie*   6
Schwitters, Kurt — *Cherry Picture*   105
Seurat, Georges — *Le Cirque (The Circus)*   59
Study for "La Grande Jatte"   36

Shao-Tang, Hsueh — *Dragon*   90
Steichen, Edward — *Moonrise—Mamaroneck, New York*   26
Tuell, Anna — *Marriage Quilt*   68
van Gogh, Vincent — *The Mulberry Tree*   49
Wright, Frank Lloyd — *Window from the Coonley Playhouse*   2

Index

A

Aboriginal art, 86, 87
Abstract Expressionism, 124
Action, showing, 116, 117
Additive sculpture, 108, 109
Advertisements, 54, 118, 119
African art, 84, 100
Albers, Anni
   Preliminary Design for Wall Hanging,
   46
American Indian art, 78, 79, 80
Animals in art, 31, 60, 61, 70, 71, 74,
   90, 130, 131
Animation, 116
Anthropologists, 84
Antonakos, Stephen
   Incomplete Neon Square for
   La Jolla, 89
Archipenko, Alexander
   The Gondolier, 109
Architects, 94
Architecture, 94, 95
Art
   Aboriginal, 86
   advertising, 54, 118, 119
   African, 84, 100
   American Indian, 78, 79, 80
   animals in, 31, 60, 61, 70, 71, 74,
      90
   Canadian Indian, 76
   careers in, 26, 32, 50, 70, 94, 98,
      111, 116, 118, 126
   elements of, listed, 1, 34, 35, 135
   galleries, 132
   materials, 104
   museums, 132

   nonobjective, 96
   Oriental, 28, 29, 74, 84, 90, 91
   shows, 132, 133
   that shows feelings, 6, 7, 35, 43, 44,
      45, 67, 96, 97, 99, 101
   that tells stories, 69, 71, 81, 97, 99,
      101, 111, 117
   as useful, 68, 69, 100
Australia, 86
Azarian, Mary
   December, 81

B

Backdrop, 62, 66
Background, 36, 37, 38, 39, 67, 92,
   93, 106, 113, 115
Balance, 34, 50, 51, 73
Bark painting, 86, 87
Bartolommeo, Fra
   Hermitage on a Slope, 39
Base, of a sculpture, 34
Batman and Robin, 116
Bearden, Romare
   Blue Interior, Morning, 1968, 104
Billboard painting, 32
Bingham, George Caleb
   Fur Traders Descending the
   Missouri, 24
Blakelock, Ralph Albert
   Moonlight, 57
Block printing, 122
Blueprints, 94, 95
Bookmaking, 99, 134
Boys Day, 40

Bralds, Braldt
  Untitled, 94
Buffalo, 31
Buildings, 16, 88, 94, 95
  creating models of, 17, 94
Butterflies, parts of, 53

C

Calendars, 80, 81
Cameras, 42
  television, 98
Canadian Indian art, 76
Cartoons, 116
Carving, 74, 75, 100
Cats, 130, 131
Cave paintings, 70
Center of interest, 58, 59, 67, 104,
  105, 131
Chalk, drawing with, 15, 43, 71, 95
Charcoal, 71
Cheyenne Indians, 80
Chinese art, 28, 74, 84, 90
Circles, 3, 15, 49, 77, 85
Clay
  printing with, 19
  sculpture, 9, 108, 109
Cloth
  designs, 84, 85, 122
  hand-woven, 46, 126
  tie-dyed, 84, 85
Clothes, 62, 64, 65
Clowns, 128, 129
Collage, 12, 13, 104, 105
Colors, 1, 3, 7, 12, 34, 38, 41, 42, 64,
  72, 77, 99, 107, 125, 127
  blending, 42, 113
  creating moods with, 44, 45
  creating unity with, 13, 15, 73

dark, 26, 27
light, 24, 25
mixing, 20, 22, 25, 27, 37
primary, 20, 21, 22, 29
secondary, 22
Color values, 25
Color wheel, 22
Comic book artists, 116
Comic strips, 116, 117
Cool colors, 44, 45
Crayons
  drawing with, 23, 24, 59, 93
  etching and, 87
  and kite making, 41
  rubbings with, 11
Cubes, 16, 19

D

Davis, Stuart
  New York Elevated, 5
Decorations
  for a building model, 17
  for a mask, 83
  pottery, 78, 79
  for a puppet, 61, 65, 129
Degas
  Little Fourteen-Year-Old Dancer, 65
Delaunay, Robert
  *Simultaneous Contrasts: Sun and
    Moon,* 37
Deserts, 112, 113, 114, 115
Designers, graphic, 118
Designs, 19, 51, 65, 78, 79, 100
  block print, 123
  with colors, 53
  fabric, 84
  kite, 41
  with lines, 5

quilling, 77
with shapes, 15
in tie-dye, 85
trademark, 119
Details, 4, 17, 35, 58, 63, 66, 89, 93, 95
Diary, 134
Diorama, 106, 107, 108
Distance, showing, 30, 31, 36, 37
Dragons, 90, 91
Drawing
a butterfly, 53
with chalk, 15, 34, 71, 95
with charcoal, 71
with crayons, 23, 47, 59, 93
lines, 5, 39, 71, 81, 117
with pencil, 5, 7, 29, 31, 41, 45, 51, 53, 57, 77, 79, 95, 115
with pens or markers, 39, 45, 81, 89, 99, 117
shapes, 15
Dunes, desert, 112

E
Egypt, 114, 115, 130
Elements of art, listed, 1, 34, 35, 135
El Greco
View of Toledo, 27
Ergs, desert, 113
Etching, crayon, 87
Exhibits, art, 133

F
Fabric, 46
collage, 12, 13
designs, 84, 85, 122

dyes, 85
patterns, 122, 123
tie-dye, 84
Fans, folding, 28, 29
Far East, the, 28
Feelings, shown in art, 6, 7, 35, 43, 44, 45, 96, 97, 99, 101
Fingerprints, 18, 55
Fish, 10
Foreground, 36, 37, 38, 39, 67, 92, 93, 115
Form, 1, 16, 34, 61, 74, 75, 94, 131
Fragonard, Jean-Honoré
The Visit to the Nursery, 45
Framing artworks, 121, 133
Frankenthaler, Helen
Small's Paradise, 96

G
Galleries, 132
Gardens, 106, 107, 108, 109
Graphic art, 118, 119
Graphic designers, 118
Guggenheim Museum, 132

H
Hasui, Kawase
Hinomisaki in Moonlight in Izumo Province, 56
Historians, 70
Horizon, 7, 113
Hopi Indians, 79
Hopper, Edward
The Long Leg, 43
Horiuchi, Paul

Mosaic Mural at the Seattle Center, 72

I

Illustrations, 111, 134
Imagination, 27, 39, 61, 102, 103, 111, 129, 131
Impressionism, 38
Indians
    Cheyenne, 80
    Hopi, 79
    Micmac, 76, 77
    Mimbres, 78
Indonesian tie-dye, 84
Ink drawings, 39

J

Jade, 74
Japanese art, 28, 40
Johnson, Eastman
    The Brown Family, 37

K

Kandinsky, Vasily
    Open Green, 14
    Painting No. 201, 21
Klee, Paul
    Cat and Bird, 131
Kites, 40, 41
Krasner, Lee
    Between Two Appearances, 97

L

Landscapes, 36
Lassaw, Ibram
    Corax, 50
Light
    and colors, 24, 25, 38, 67
    moonlight, 26, 56, 57
Lindstrand, Doug
    Untitled, 71
Lines, 1, 3, 9, 34, 85, 99, 129
    balance and, 50
    drawing with, 5, 39, 71, 81, 117
    kinds of, 4, 5, 6, 7
    and movement, 116, 117
    and sculpture, 8, 50, 51
    and signatures, 6
Looms, weaving, 125
Louvre, the, 132

M

Magic window, making a , 2, 3, 34
Masks, 82, 83
Media, artists', 87, 103, 131
Merriam, Eve
    "Landscape," 110
Metropolitan Museum of Art, 132
Mexican art, 7, 82
Micmac Indians, 76, 77
Mimbres Indians, 78
Models, building, 17, 94
Molds, sculpture, 9
Mondrian, Piet
    Composition, V., 14
Monet, Claude
    Cliffs of Pourville, Morning, 38
Monochromatic pictures, 42, 43
Moods, creating, in artworks, 6, 7, 35, 43, 44, 45, 67, 96, 97, 99, 101

Moonlight, 56, 57
Moore, Henry
  Figures in a Setting, 44
Mosaics, 72, 73, 88
Mounting artworks, 121, 133
Movement, showing, 116, 117
Murals, 88, 102, 113
Museum of Fine Arts, Boston, 133

N
Naha, Helen
  Hopi Wedding Vase, 79
Names, making pictures of, 6
Nampeyo, Rachel
  Hopi Jar, 78
Nearikas, Mexican, 7
Neon, 89
Nile, the, 114
Nonobjective art, 96, 97

O
Oases, desert, 112, 114
Oldenburg, Claes
  Geometric Mouse Scale A, 88
  Screwarch Bridge, 102
Oriental art, 28, 29, 74, 84, 90, 91
Ouchi, Michi
  Hanabi (Fireworks), 84
Oval, 93
Overlapping, 13, 21, 30, 31, 43, 55,
  59, 107

P
Paint, using
  with crayons, 41
  to mix colors, tints, and shades, 25,
    27, 43, 57
  for pictures, 27, 37, 43, 57, 66, 113,
    125
  for printing, 19, 55, 123
  for puppets, 61, 63, 65, 91
  to show feelings, 45, 97
Painting, styles of, 101, 135
  Abstract Expressionism, 124
  bark, 86
  cave, 70
  Impressionism, 38
  nonobjective, 97
  spatter, 125
Paper, ways of folding, 3, 24, 29, 47,
  129
Papier-mâché, 62, 63, 90, 91
Parrott, Alice
  La Mesa, 12
Patterns, 12, 13, 64, 65, 122, 127
Perspective, 30, 31, 33, 35, 36, 38,
  39, 57, 58, 59
Peru, 82
Photographers, 26
Photographs, 26, 42, 58, 111
Picasso, Pablo
  Three Musicians, 135
Plans, for artworks, 11, 23, 46, 47, 131
Plaster, 74, 75
Plateaus, desert, 112
Plays, 62
  puppet, 62-66
Poems, 110
Pollock, Jackson
  Number 1, 1950 (Lavender Mist),
    124
Portfolio, artist's, 100
Portraits, 89, 92, 93
Posters, 54, 118
Pottery, American Indian, 78, 79

Primary colors, 20, 21, 29
Printing, 18, 19
 block, 122, 123
 with clay, 19
 with stencils, 120, 121
 thumbprints, 55
Prutscher, Otto
 Wine Goblet, 68
Puppeteers, 64
Puppet play, putting on a, 66
Puppets, 61, 62, 63, 128, 129
 making clothes for, 65
Pyramids, the, 114

Q
Quilling, 76, 77
Quilts, 69

R
Redon, Odilon
 Vase of Flowers, 23
Rhythm, 12, 34, 55, 121, 123, 127
Roles, in plays, 62, 63, 65
Rubbings, 10, 11
Ruscha, Ed
 Annie, 6

S
Sahara, the, 112, 113, 114, 115
Scales, fish, 10
Schwitters, Kurt
 Cherry Picture, 105
Scraps, art from, 13, 17, 68, 104, 105
Sculpture, 8, 9

additive, 108, 109
animal, 61, 74
Chinese, 74, 75
clay, 9, 108, 109
large, 88
lines and, 8, 50, 51
metal, 65, 74, 109
papier-mâché, 63, 90, 91
plaster, 75
soft, 61, 131
stone, 8
wire, 51
Self-portraits, 89, 92, 93
Seurat, Georges
 Le Cirque (The Circus), 59
 Study for "La Grande Jatte", 36
Shades, 27, 43, 57
Shao-Tang, Hsueh
 Dragon, 90
Shapes, 1, 3, 14, 15, 16, 34, 41, 83, 99, 129
Silhouettes, 89
Space, 50, 57, 59, 109, 113, 121
Spatter painting, 125
Sphinx, the, 114
Spirals, 48, 49
Squares, 3, 15
Steichen, Edward
 Moonrise, Mamaroneck, New York, 26
Stencils, 120, 121
Storyboard, 99
Symbols, 78, 79, 90, 93, 119
Symmetry, 52, 53, 67
Syria, 73

T
Television, 98, 99

cartoons, 116
  producers, 98, 99
  shows, making, 99
Texture, 1, 9, 34, 35, 67, 129
  of cloth, 13, 65
  and collage, 12, 13
  lines and, 8
  rubbings and, 10, 11
  in sculpture, 8
Three-dimensional objects, 16, 94
Thumbprints, 54
Tie-dye, 84, 85
Tints, 24, 25, 37, 43
Titling artworks, 23, 31, 57, 105
Trademarks, 119
Triangles, 3, 15

U
Unicorn, 61
Unity in art, 12, 13, 15, 72, 73

V
Value, color, 1, 25
van Gogh, Vincent
  The Mulberry Tree, 49
Variety in art, 54, 55
Vessels, ancient Chinese, 74

W
Warm colors, 44, 45, 129
Warp, 47
Weaving, 46, 47, 122, 126, 127
Weft, 47
Winter counts, 80
Wright, Frank Lloyd
  *Window from the Coonley
    Playhouse,* 2

Acknowledgments

We gratefully acknowledge the valuable contributions of the following artists, consultants, editorial advisors, and reviewers who participated in the development of this book: Ruth Jones and C.J. Greenwald, teachers, St. Luke's Lutheran Day School, La Mesa, CA; Mirta Golino, art educator and editorial advisor, San Diego; Jeff Jurich, animator and writer, Celluloid Studios, Denver; Dennis Smith, sculptor, Highland, UT; Virginia Gadzala, costume designer, San Diego; Phyllis Thurston, former Art Supervisor, Pinellas County School District, Clearwater, FL; Judy Chicago and Mary Ross Taylor, Through the Flower, Benicia, CA; Andrew Blanks, Jr., art teacher, Johnston Middle School, Houston; Barbara Pearson Roberts, teacher, Sabal Palm Elementary School, Tallahassee; Shirley and Terry McManus, puppetry consultants, "Puppets Please," San Diego; Dr. Wayne Woodward, associate professor of art education, Georgia Southwestern College; Mary Riggs of Riggs Galleries, San Diego; Anna Ganahl, Director of Public Relations, Art Center College of Design, Pasadena; Françoise Gilot, artist, La Jolla, CA; Leven C. Leatherbury, independent consultant in art education, San Diego; Betty Cavanaugh, curriculum consultant in art education, Upland, CA; Joel Hagen, artist and writer, Oakdale, CA; Kellene Champlin, Art Supervisor, Fulton County Schools, Atlanta; Mar Gwen Land, art teacher, Montgomery Jr. High School, San Diego; LaRene McGregor, fiber artist, McKenzie Bridge, OR; Norma Wilson, former art teacher and editorial advisor, San Diego; Dr. Ann S. Richardson, Supervisor of Art, Foreign Languages, and Gifted and Talented Education, Charles County Public Schools, LaPlata, MD; Talli Larrick, educator and writer, El Cajon, California; Mary Apuli, Coordinator of Elementary Program, Indiana School District No. 16, Minneapolis; Carol Widdop-Sonka, artist and writer, San Diego; Virginia Fitzpatrick, art educator and writer, Bloomington, IN; Evelyn Ackerman, artist, Era Industries, Culver City, CA; Judy Kugel, teacher trainer for Learning to Read Through the Arts, New York City; Arlie Zolynas, educator and author, San Diego; Nancy Remington, Principal, Sacramento Country Day School, Sacramento; Kay Alexander, Art Consultant, Palo Alto School District, Palo Alto, CA; Billie Phillips, Lead Art Supervisor, St. Louis Public Schools, St. Louis; Sister Marie Albert, S.S.J., Principal, St. Callistus School, Philadelphia; Robert Vickery, artist, Orleans, MA.

We especially appreciate the students from the following schools who contributed the student art reproduced in this series: O.H. Anderson Elem. School, Mahtomedi, MN; Atkinson Elem. School, Barnesville, MN; W.D. Hall Elem. School, El Cajon, CA; Idlewild Elem. School, Memphis, TN; Irving Elem. School, St. Louis, MO; MacArthur Elem. School, Indianapolis, IN; Oakwood Elem. School, Knoxville, TN; John Roe Elem. School, St. Louis, MO; Taylors Falls School District #140, Taylors Falls, MN; Washington Elem. School, Pomona, CA; Enterprise Elem. School, Enterprise, FL; Kellogg Elem. School, Chula Vista, CA; Learning to Read Through the Arts, New York, NY; Lewis School, San Diego, CA; Woodcrest Elem. School, Fridley, MN; Westwood Elem. School, San Diego, CA; Independent School District #16, Minneapolis, MN; St. Luke's Lutheran Day School, La Mesa, CA; Country Day School, Sacramento, CA; Budd School, Fairmont, MN; Park Terrace Elem. School, Spring Lake Park, MN; Audubon Elem. School, Baton Rouge, LA; Chilowee Elem. School, Knoxville, TN; Logan Elem. School, San Diego, CA; Grassy Creek Elem. School, Indianapolis, IN; Earle Brown Elem. School, Brooklyn Center, MN; Jefferson Elem. School, Winona, MN; Calvert Elem. School, Prince Frederick, MD; Barnsville Elem. School, Barnsville, MN; Ridgedale Elem. School, Knoxville, TN; Children's Creative and Performing Arts Academy, San Diego, CA; Steven V. Correia School, San Diego, CA; Walnut Park Elem. School, St. Louis, MO.

Although it is impossible to acknowledge all the contributors to this project, we express special thanks for the generous efforts of the following individuals: Janet Reim, Gail Kozar, Rae Murphy, Jan Thompson, Gerald Williams, Timothy Asfazadour, Judy Cannon, Helen Negley, Crystal Thorson, Rachelle and Tyler Bruford, Mary Bluhm, David Zielinski, David Oliver, Daniel and Carl Bohman, Anne G. Allen, Bao Vuong, Gail W. Guth, Signe Ringbloom, Claire Murphy, Joan Blaine, Patrice M. Sparks, and Larke Johnston.

Coronado Staff: Marsha Barrett Lippincott, Level 1 Editor; Janet Kylstad Coulon, Level 2 Editor; Deanne Kells Cordell, Level 3 Editor; Carol Spirkoff Prime, Level 4 Editor; Patricia McCambridge, Level 5 Editor; DeLynn Decker, Level 6 Editor; Janis Heppell, Project Designer; Lisa Peters, Designer; Myrtali Anagnostopoulos, Designer; Debra Saleny, Photo Research.